What people are saying abou

It's rare to find a book that covers the practical realities of life in the music business from the musician's perspective, while also keeping the magic of music front and center.

This fine book does both and it's an absolute must for student musicians, though I dare say, seasoned pros will love it too. I also recommend it to non-musicians who really love music.

Music and Life will add to your appreciation of your favorite artists by giving you an understanding of behind-the-scenes trials and challenges every musician must overcome on their heroic journey to becoming and surviving as professional musicians.

—Ken McCarthy,
Jazz on the Tube

For as long as I can remember, I've been an admirer of Mike Vaccaro's professionalism, musicianship, insight and honesty. *Music and Life* is an invaluable resource for aspiring musicians and for seasoned professionals alike. Whether you are a performer, teacher, and/or involved in music commerce, you will greatly benefit from Mike's vast experience and success in the music industry. Congratulations and thank you for sharing your knowledge and wisdom!

—Clarence Padilla
Professor of Clarinet, Drake University
Des Moines Symphony Orchestra

I always encourage artists to find their authentic selves. It's easy to copy another person; finding your true self is challenging. The audience will always immediately recognize and praise the one that made the effort.

—Irma de Jong
Executive Director
iClassical-Academy.com
www.iClassical-Academy.com

Being the stepparent of a clarinet player, I'd love to see this book, *Music and Life*, in the hands of the parents of every woodwind students. I didn't have a clue about the instrument, the reeds I bought, etc. I wish I'd known more and have been able to be more supportive. I took piano and guitar lessons and knew nothing about woodwinds. I also love the nuggets of wisdom you sprinkle throughout the book, Mike. A treasure!

—Marian Hartsough
PublishingforPublicity.com

MUSIC AND LIFE

THOUGHTS ON MUSIC, PHRASING, WOODWINDS AND THIS MODERN WORLD

MIKE VACCARO

ADC MEDIA
Amore del Cuore

MUSIC AND LIFE

Thoughts on Music, Phrasing,
Woodwinds and This Modern World

Copyright 2024 Mike Vaccaro

Published by ADC Media

ISBN: 979-8-218-24509-2

Printed in the United States of America

ADC MEDIA
www.mikevaccaro.com

Acknowledgments

Where do I start? So many people have helped me in this life. The beginning seems like the best place to start. My parents Tony and Eunice Vaccaro always let me find out about life on my own, while watching me to make sure I didn't hurt myself or get in with the wrong group of people.

Then there were my music teachers, Stan Seckler, Leon Guide, Robert Sonner, Robert Strecker, John Jacobs, Ralph Gari, Luella Howard, Maestro Henry Temianka, and many others with whom I only took a few lessons. And many thanks go to my friends who were also my teachers, teaching me both good as well as a few harmful things.

Also, there were many musicians and music contractors who hired me throughout my life. Thank You.

I also want to thank the many musicians who befriended me and taught me so much throughout my career, in addition to all the musicians I hired at the Cerritos Center for the Performing Arts, who were absolutely the cream of the Los Angeles area crop. Thanks for being on time and playing so great. You represented me well.

I want to thank the many people from the years when I put music aside to produce events for America's largest corporations and the production companies that hired me. That was a huge business lesson. Another lesson I appreciated was being a Union official in two separate Musicians' Locals. I learned the art of negotiation there.

And a special thanks to all the composers who not only hired me for their motion pictures but also wrote such great music for my 10 CDs in various styles. Plus, thanks to all the musicians who played and help bring the music to life on those CDs.

I am grateful for all the instrument technicians who kept my horns in shape and made mouthpieces for me.

Thanks Bill Stevens, for our endeavor into barrel and bell making for the clarinet, and Rhueben Allen for our venture into the AV Clarinet line and his friendship with me. Then I must add Glen Johnston, Marc Yacoubian, John Reilly, and John Yoakum, who helped me with the art of making mouthpieces and the voodoo inherent in that art.

My three wives and a three-year domestic partner taught me much about life, but it is my lovely third wife, Rosemary, who has not only loved me, but has helped me greatly in so many ways. Save the best for last.

Now my thanks go out to Marian Hartsough who knows the book business from many years of experience. Thanks to her I now know the difference between a noun and a verb. She also helped with spelling and made sure this book could be read so you could understand the words. With the many quotes in the book, she was dead serious about making sure all the sources were correct. I also want to thank her for her knowledge of how to get the book published and placed in various markets. Experience counts and Ms. Hartsough has the expertise.

If I have forgotten to mention you, please know that I love you and appreciate you as I do all my true friends.

Contents

PART TWO: EZINES   93

PART THREE: A BROADER LOOK AT LIFE'S PROBLEMS   271

Preface

I have read many used books that could easily pass for being brand new...Pristine. No underlines, no circled text, and nothing written in the margins. That tells me that the reader probably did not take any notes as he or she went through the material. I have always thought that reading, like music, should be interactive, so unless you got your copy from the library, I encourage you to take notes in the margins of this book, and on any other blank spaces you can find. It's a great way to mark the salient parts, as well as your own thoughts as you read.

The same is true for written music. When I'm working on a piece of music, it looks like a jumble of written marks to me—a big "P" where I want it soft or an accidental after I have missed a note a few times—reminders of phrasing. Try it and see if it works for you.

You'll be glad you did!

I urge you to read this book slowly. Read a subject and think about it. After you've digested a point and made your own decisions about the validity of what I have said, then move on to the next idea.

Be Eager to Learn

Introduction

I was born Michael Anthony Vaccaro in Los Angeles, California, U.S.A. Most people call me Mike and that's what I prefer. For those of you who know Los Angeles, I was born at was called back then Mothers' Hospital near the SoFi Stadium. For the first four years of my life, I lived near the 5 Freeway and Soto St. Then we moved to the suburbs, which at that time were a few blocks of houses in the middle of miles and miles of orange groves.

Let me say right now that I had wonderful parents who cared for me and loved me greatly. *There is nothing more important for adulthood than having had a great childhood.* I wish that for every single person on this planet, even though we all know it's not always that way. A great childhood gives the young man or woman an advantage in life, simply because they're not fighting demons taught to them by their parents. Make no mistake, we are all a product of our parents and carry not only their DNA throughout our lives, but also inherit their manner of thinking and managing life.

We were not rich. My dad was a welder and my mom a secretary. We had enough to live on in a comfortable way, though, and even have dinner out on payday.

So, I lived a good life amongst the orange groves, although they were soon cut down, and did the things kids did in the 1950s, like exploring, dirt clod fights, orange fights, and watching the big train come by while we gorged on wild blackberries and raspberries.

Then it happened.

In fourth grade, the junior high school band played for an assembly and I was mesmerized. It was my first experience with live music. Then we were asked to come up to the stage if we were interested in playing an instrument. Of course I was. I wanted to play the trumpet.

Well, to my chagrin the band director said he already had too many trumpet players and that I should play the clarinet. I was mortally wounded. The clarinet? Really? So, I took up the clarinet. It wasn't until many years later that I realized it was a blessing in disguise because I would never have had the attitude necessary to play the trumpet. The clarinet fitted me perfectly, as did the rest of the wood-winds that would enter my life as I progressed.

My parents bought me Benny Goodman and Sol Yaged recordings to introduce to me to the sound of the clarinet. My first teacher was "Johnny the Barber," who taught at the local music store, and was, in fact, my barber. A nice man, but not the right teacher. There was another teacher at the store by the name of Stan Seckler who then became my teacher until I went to college. He played in the local Civic Light Opera orchestra and had a lot of strong opinions on music and musicians.

Was I a good student? I don't know, but I seemed to be the best student he had. My formula for preparing for my lessons was to do nothing most of the week, and then for the last couple of days before the lesson, learn the music just well enough that most of the time he would let me progress to the next section of my study book. He had a funny quirk of pounding on my leg when I didn't play the lesson at tempo. Many times, because of my practice habits, I couldn't play it in a steady tempo because I was just trying to get through it.

The conductor of the junior high school band turned out to be my elementary school band teacher. He came once a week. As far as I'm concerned, he and the other elementary school teachers were all angels. He drove a beautiful Chrysler Imperial and admitted to me many years later that he'd really wanted a Cadillac, he made good money playing jobs on the weekends, but he didn't want to upset the other teachers.

Once I was walking to the car with him and asked him what was the most important thing to do in music. *"Be good at more than one thing,"* was his advice. Thank you, Leon Guide! Those words were to inspire me for my whole career, *and* they encouraged me to be interested in a lot of things—both in music and in life.

All through my life, my parents helped me with extracurricular activities and let me pursue them until I was no longer interested. I didn't really excel in music, but I did play the first chair in the elementary and middle school bands. I also added the saxophone to my repertoire of instruments just before high school.

In high school, I tried all the available sports in the first couple of years and became a bit disinterested in music. So, I told my parents they should stop giving me music lessons because I wasn't really interested.

Then it happened again.

I was at Disneyland in the front row when the Count Basie band played with their great lead alto player, Marshall Royal. That was it. Not only did I want private lessons again, but I knew music was how I was going to try and make my living.

So, I went back to my parents and told them that I was really interested in music again and could I take private lessons once more. "Of course, you can, Son, but this time you're going to have to pay for the lessons yourself. We paid for them until you weren't interested anymore, and now that you are interested again, it's best you pay for them yourself." Talk about a big life lesson. I think this was the biggest lesson I had learned thus far in my life.

Well, there was that time I lied to my dad and I got the spanking of all time (that was allowed in those days). *And a good lesson it was.* Always speak the truth to people who deserve it. And certainly, my great parents deserved it.

High school was going well. Robert Strecker was band director of our marching band, 16-strong and better sounding than some 80-piece bands. No dead weight in that band of high school kids! It was amazing how a small band playing in tune and together can sound better than an 80-piece band with a lot of dead wood in it.

In my sophomore year, the band got bigger and better, and we even had a jazz band. I met some musicians who I was sure would be going into the music business, but they decided on other ways to make a living. I understand. They were fun to play with, though, and I learned a lot from them.

I was still with Stan Seckler as a private teacher. Now that I was the one paying, I was practicing on a regular basis, and sometimes for a good amount of time. I was serious now. I was going to be a musician and I was going to college in two years. The world was changing. At that point, I also started playing the flute.

My junior year of high school went well and I was able to prepare a couple of solos for the solo festivals. Then suddenly, I was a senior with a new great band director, John Jacobs from Colorado. And now I was half of a drum major team and so happy not to have the horn jumping around in my mouth while I tried to get my leg parallel to the ground. Yuk! Concert band season was great and Mr. Jacobs really knew his literature.

Graduation time came, and I had to make a college choice. My father, who was a welder in a steel mill and smoked two packs of Chesterfields, was on the last leg of cancer. He'd had cancer for the four years I was in high school—a classic research specimen. Oddly enough, lung cancer is still one of the toughest to cure to this day. They burnt my dad to death. A few days after my graduation, which he could not attend, he died.

This changed my thinking about college. Junior college seemed much easier on me and my sweet mother. And it turned out to be a great choice. I met my new private instructor, Ralph Gari, who knew the clarinet and saxophone classical literature—and became my second father figure. I played in Ralph's Sax Quartet many years later and we made a wonderful record of some of the most difficult and most beautiful music in the literature.

The music department was very forward thinking and started a group called the Collegiate Neophonic, which were two separate bands of the best young musicians in the whole Los Angeles area. It was based on Stan Kenton's Neophonic Orchestra. *Really great music.* We ended up going to Miami for a music festival and received many kudos. And each of the members went on to an illustrious career in the music business.

After junior college, it was off to a four-year music school. I keep my private teacher, Ralph Gari, and attended an institution that really didn't even recognize jazz as valid. So, being the industrious students we were, we started a jazz band at the dinner hour when the teachers were not around. After winning at a jazz festival, the music department had to accept jazz as music. They went on to start one of the first commercial music courses in California.

In addition, the orchestra conductor was the brilliant virtuoso, Henry Temianka, who was one of the founders of the Paganini String Quartet—all playing on Stradivarius instruments. He was also the director of the California Chamber Symphony. What a joy to be playing for a professional of the highest level. And he liked to go to the corner bar and have a beer with some of the orchestra members too. I learned so much from him about professional standards—I am appreciative to this day.

And then it happened once more.

Having been a recipient of a scholarship to attend the university, I was selected by Maestro Temianka to perform the *Scaramouche* for Alto Sax and Orchestra by Darius Milhaud with composer Milhaud in attendance. The concert was attended by the French Embassy and was the West Coast premiere of the composition.

I must explain the routines I used for learning music and later on in business. Since almost everything I did was new to me, besides my regular practice, I would find out what needed to be learned, and then I would work hard on it for hours a day until I owned it.

Soon after I performed the *Scaramouche*, my contacts from the Collegiate Neophonic were helpful in getting me employment with the

Stan Kenton Band. Stan becomes my second surrogate father. I called him the "Big White Father."

I stayed with the Kenton band for four years, with a couple of side tours with Woody Herman and with the Paul Horn Concert Ensemble (*flute quartet and rhythm section*).

I could tell you many road stories; however, I feel more comfortable keeping them to myself. Let me just say that it was an education in both music and interpersonal relationships. I must say that it was very different from being on the road in the 21st century, with touring buses and first-class treatment everywhere you go.

We lived on a Greyhound bus and spent most nights traveling to the next gig (*job*) with someone in the wheel well to make sure the bus driver didn't fall asleep on a mountain road. No google maps, just the old paper state map. We got to every job on time.

Thanks, Dennis Justice, for keeping a straight line on the road. You always got us there. You were also helpful in getting the band set up and selling albums at the job. And your driving was superb. Dennis ended up working in the office for the Kenton Organization and then went with the Willard Alexander booking agency, one of the top agencies in the United States. He is still a close friend.

Staying in a hotel was a luxury. Generally, about half the time was spent on overnight bus trips. The first year I was on the Kenton band, we worked 363 days straight before a day off in Manhattan, Kansas. Think of a week like this all on the bus: Chicago, NYC, Chicago, Boston, Chicago, NYC, and again Chicago. Stinky . . . besides all the other problems. Get off the bus, do the job, get back on the bus, on to the next job, etc.

I ended my road wanderlust in Las Vegas with the Kenton band. In those days, the union was very powerful and I had to wait six months to get a union card. Most of the time, I would come back to LA and stay with mom while driving up to Las Vegas to sign in at the union once a week. At this time, I started learning the oboe, which kept me in the music business when the business was slow.

I spent a year with the Si Zentner band at the Tropicana, working on the Follies Bergère Show. Just to let you know how the thinking was in Las Vegas in those days, the entrance to the pit was through the women's dressing room. Seeing a woman naked was a common occurrence and very impersonal. Everyone was just doing their job.

After a year of the same show two times a night, six nights a week, I couldn't take it any longer and went back to LA for rest and relaxation. A couple of months later I got a call to work at the Sands in a celebrity showroom. At the time, the Sands was one of the three major hotels that had the top entertainment. I got to play with Sammy Davis Jr., Lena Horne, and many of the top performers of the day. I did that job for two and a half years while also playing with the Las Vegas Symphony, The Las Vegas Chamber Orchestra (modern music), and kix bands at the union from 2–5 AM. I still like to stay up late, but usually by 1 AM or so I give up.

We also had a small chamber group and performed concerts for schools all over Nevada. It was an amazing experience playing in small towns and enjoying the chance to see terrain and cities with stories that most people never hear about.

After the Sands, I was very tired of desert living. With my new wife, Judith Dunlore, a fabulous classical soprano vocalist, we decided to try Europe. I had a job offer in Germany, so we ended up in Munich, a gorgeous city with three opera houses and three full-time orchestras. The first night we were there, we couldn't get a ticket to any of the venues, as they were all sold out.

I did a motion picture with the ones who hired me, but there seemed to be some discomfort from their side about me, and I certainly didn't enjoy the experience, so we moved on with a cordial goodbye. I did get friendly with a few of the woodwind players, and we kept in touch for the several months we were in Germany. Judith found out that we were there at the wrong time for the opera auditions, so we decided to see Europe.

We traveled south as far as Sorrento, Italy and north as far as Oslo,

Norway, where I had friends. Europe is such a beautiful place, and Germany especially was a pleasure with all the music that was available—and its beautiful countryside.

Europeans seemed much more relaxed than Americans. We stopped at a very small town in the Alps where there was a parade, and all the townspeople were there with everyone dressed in traditional German garb. The musicians in the parade were dressed so colorfully and played well. We asked one of the people what the occasion was, and he said, "We have so many holidays, I don't seem to know what this one is." That's living.

After our European adventure, we came back to the U.S. and faced a situation where neither my wife nor I could find work. She started teaching and I started practicing. We faced a year of not performing. Then something happened. I was at the union building one day and heard this great classical pianist, Jack Reidling. His wife was the Union Secretary and pretty much ran the whole union. She didn't drive, so Jack took her to work and home every day. Lucky for us, he was there at the same time I was. I talked him into going through some music that I had and then Judith did the same. Soon we had a great trio. We rehearsed three days a week for six hours. After a year, we gave our first concert and recorded our first CD, *Caprice*.

I learned what it takes to be prepared. We all could play our parts without even thinking. *The notes were in us.* We owned the music. We played on the Columbia Artists Community Concerts, just as that series started winding down. And we played radio broadcasts from the County Museum. Every few months, we would play a local concert. But the best part was rehearsing and learning the literature well enough to own it.

After many years my wife and I split, and the trio ended up being part of the breakup. That group was called "Musique." It was, and is, the musical highlight of my life, despite all the other great experiences I have had.

While we had the trio, I had to work to make a living, of course, so

I will tell you what happened over the next few years, although I can't remember the chronological order: I worked in a dinner theater with an excellent trio and the keyboard player did all the cut-down arrangements—keyboards, woodwinds, and percussion. It sounded big. I think this was about the time I was teaching at the University of California, Irvine. During that period, I was also a Union official in two separate jurisdictions and was on the negotiation committee for most contracts.

Additionally, I played in The Long Beach Opera for 10 years. I started the first few operas on English horn, and when the principal clarinet chair became open, I switched to that chair. We performed the classic opera repertoire and some well-selected contemporary operas. We also performed *The Ring* (four Wagner Operas) with the cut-down instrumentation with no substitutions in any section. All four operas were performed on Saturday and Sunday. Every member said it took a week to get over it because it was so tiring. I was also working as an added member of the Pacific Symphony and LA Philharmonic.

At about this time, I was getting tired of doing seven shows a week, for weeks on end, many weeks of boredom, although they paid very well.

When I was contracting the band for The Rams football team—on the 0-yard line of the field—dangerous for sure—Lois Arata, who worked for Jack Morton Productions, asked me if I would be interested in providing production services for them. This became the start of an 8- to 10-year hiatus from full-time playing. I provided music and entertainment, including Celebrity Entertainment, and provided my orchestra for accompaniment, dinner music, and dance music after the show. I also provided sound, lights, staging, themed events, and audio-visual backup when required.

Jack Morton had an office in almost every big city in the United States, and I became the go-to person for any of these offices coming to California and even Mexico. Ray Bloch Productions also started using me, and that was a very interesting business education. I found out California is a really big place, as we worked up and down the state, in Nevada a bit, and even occasionally in Mexico. I also started representing a symphony pops conductor, as if I wasn't busy enough.

After several years in that business, I went back to Broadway shows at bigger venues. And during this time, I started to be called for Motion Pictures. After a while, the picture business was my main income. I played mostly solo clarinet and a few doubles, if required. Pixar movies were a big part of my motion business income.

I retired at 65, and thought I would sit around, read books, take vacations, and be a successful geezer. But it was not to be. I could not give up music. I wasn't using it to make a living, but I found out music was my religion, so I have been making CDs and DVDs with various groups, both in jazz and classical formats.

I think while I'm alive, at least, they will be housed on my website **www.mikevaccaro.com**, where you can sign on for my bi-monthly blog or at **www.CiceroneMusicandArt.com**.

Life has been, and continues to be, a wild ride. I seem busier than ever. I have a feeling that time is the same, but it is I who has slowed down—just a bit.

I hope you enjoy this book and get something out of it that helps your life.

As I say in my bi-monthly blog and in this book:

> **"Be happy where you are at while you**
> **are trying to get where you want to be."**

Being happy, even with all the problems that are thrown at us, is just a decision to be happy. Even if bad things happen. It is a choice you make to be happy.

Ciao,

Mike Vaccaro / 2024

PART ONE

Music, Teaching, Woodwinds and Money

Part One is mostly about woodwind playing. However, it does include many ideas that are suitable for any musician to read. Even if the article is directed at woodwind musicians, all musicians will understand what I am saying and will be able to relate it to their own instrument. Parts Two and Three are written so any musician will be able to take something from the content, as they are universally discussed problems about the art of learning music.

CHAPTER 1

Secrets

Well now, if you are only going to read part of this dissertation, **this is the section for you.**

These ideas, I am sure, will be proffered and enhanced in the following pages, however, they deserve their own early consideration.

The first and foremost rule for me for the past 25 years (I wish it were 60) has been:

> **Be happy with where you are while you
> are trying to get to where you want to be.**

(You will see this repeated many times in this book. . . . It is *that* important).

It's easy to be impatient. One must remember that music, art, and in fact, life itself, is a lifetime of growth and experience.

Someone once said to me that "type A personalities are the only people that get anything done." I don't want to debate the truth of that statement here. I do know that it takes an incredible amount of time, dedication, and energy to do anything at a proficient level (especially in the discipline of music), and even more to take that proficiency to the level of "art."

It's easy to be impatient.

Let's remember too that art is a spirit and can exist whether one is a musician, painter, gardener, auto mechanic, or student of life. In short, "art" is available to everyone based on attitude. Art is thus available to all of us with a good level of proficiency. However, "high art" requires the art spirit *and* proficiency.

One of the greatest artists I ever encountered was a gardener at a hotel I was staying at in Phoenix, Arizona in the mid-1970s. He tended the courtyard

Art is available to everyone.

daily to create one of the most beautiful environments I have ever seen. I think he knew every blade of grass, every leaf, and every living thing in the courtyard intimately and with love.

Some people "get it" sooner than others, but no one is exempt from the journey or the growth that music, art, and life provide. You will want to read a book called *The Art Spirit* by Robert Henri. At the time of this writing, it is still available.

So, if we are patient, and if we can plan a focused and consistent method of practice and/or training, we can then settle into a pace of improvement and growth that is most beneficial to our own mental health.

The most essential idea in a music study period, for example, is to **practice one minute a day**. Just one minute minimum, but do it every day. If you want to play a little more, all the better.

It's also wise not to say the word *practice* to students, which has a terrible denotation. It's better to say *study, learn, play,* or some other more acceptable word. Flow with the stream. Some days you will go a little slowly, and other days you will not want to stop.

> **Practice is not linear, even for professionals.**
> **One day to the next, one hour to the next,**
> **all aspects can fluctuate significantly. It is normal.**

This is not to say that intense and long hours of practice are not necessary or are harmful. Most musicians I know, in addition to their long-term habit of regular methodic practice, have had periods of intense practice with long hours in the practice room.

The trick then is to work (or play) in a manner that's not obsessive or compulsive or injurious to ourselves. That is, to have a goal *and* to be happy with our consistent journey to that goal. Remember that art is a lifelong road.

In study, we start almost everything slowly and increase the speed to an appropriate tempo. Why is that?

Simple but important!

We must train our bodies *slowly* to make sure our movements are pure and not wasted motion. When this idea becomes our mantra, we gain complete control of all aspects of playing.

> *Good musicians practice slowly,*
> *and great musicians practice even slower.*
> — James Moody

> *Practice is like a sponge.*
> *Put the sponge in and out of water quickly*
> *and the sponge doesn't get completely wet.*
> *Leave the sponge in the water long enough*
> *and it will be completely wet.*
> *Practice is much the same.*
> — Itzhak Pearlman

Since goals change in midstream and are replaced with new goals once we achieve them, it makes sense to stay the course and "in the moment."

This *in the moment idea* is easier on our self-esteem. It helps to keep us from beating ourselves up for who we are not.

If we wanted to be a genius, a Mozart or Bach, we would be there already. For most of us mortals, the steady study path is best.

Remember:
Success is getting what you want, and
happiness is wanting what you get.

Another favorite axiom of mine is:

We become what we practice on a daily basis!

So:

If you practice music on a daily basis, you are *a musician*.

If you paint on a daily basis, you are *a painter*.

If you drink on a daily basis, you are *an alcoholic*.

If you train physically on a daily basis, you are *an athlete*.

If you overeat on a daily basis, you are *fat*.

You get the idea!

To attain success in either the business of music or in the art of music, it's very helpful that you enjoy learning. Again, as always, the same is true in life.

BECOME A PRACTICING MACHINE
Practice does not make perfect.
Only perfect practicing makes perfect.
—Vince Lombardi

You can read all the textbooks,
and listen to all the records,
but you have to play with musicians
that are better than you.
— Stan Getz

Yet another secret:

Save Your Money!!!

Unless you are born into money, it drops from the sky, or you live in a monastery—money, how to use money, and how to keep money are crucial skills to develop. Most likely you did not learn those skills in school. If your family didn't teach you about money, get a financial advisor, and watch people with money, and how they handle their money. Be frugal. Buy everything that you need but don't buy two or three of them. Don't buy things that you don't need and are going to end up in your garage or the trash or at some used item store. Dress well, but not above your means. **And most important is for you to write your money plan down.** How much are you going to save, how, how much for transportation, a place to live, and what you are going to give to charity, etc.?

It becomes a pie chart but starts with writing in longhand what your thoughts are about success, your money, and your life. The pie chart becomes a picture of your money, and how you are going to use it.

Pay yourself first, before any bills you may have. And try to live without debt whenever possible, unless it's making money for you. Like a home. You can put the money in a bank or bury it in your backyard. Please don't use that as specu-

> **It is imperative that you write your plans down.**

lation money. The only reason to use that money is to purchase a house if it's affordable to you. Then continue to save and make any improvements in your house from another part of the money from your written plans. If you don't write your plans down, it ruminates in your mind forever with concrete decisions seldom made.

BREATH

Everything that is about brass and woodwind playing is predicated on one thing: **Breath.** Life is predicated on breath too, though most times you don't notice it. It affects every aspect of your playing—volume, equipment, style, and literally every aspect of your performance. And how you interact with other musicians you play or work with depends on your equipment and your understanding of the importance of being able to manipulate your sound via airflow.

Especially with beginners, breath is so important.

It has been my experience that those beginners who play with very little breath seem to be introverted, and I have found it very difficult to coerce them into playing louder no matter what exercises or thinking on the subject I offer to them. With enough indoctrination over a few years, they mostly end up with a robust tone and an even more outgoing personality. Sometimes changing their equipment to a harder reed or a more open mouthpiece can hasten this change.

Then there is the beginner who plays loud all the time. This is particularly true of the natural athlete who has an advanced respiratory system. This is an easier problem to fix, as one only has to put their arms around the sound to mitigate the harshness of playing. The equipment might need to be changed or perhaps not.

In either case, some of that comes from the equipment they start with, whether purchased or rented, or the ignorance of aftermarket products to help them change their plight for the better.

Even advanced musicians must realize the importance of air to achieve the many playing styles they will come across. Someone who plays sweetly uses their air completely differently than a robust player. Take a piece of the solo literature and listen to five to ten recordings and you will likely hear five to ten variables in sound, concept, and delivery.

Any qualified teacher understands that teaching, especially for beginners, psychology is as important as teaching notes and rhythm. The young student has many hurdles to overcome to continue with the long journey to be an accomplished musician. All along the way, from the beginning to the advanced student, the psyche of the student must be understood. Yes, we can only teach music, but it is based on our understanding of how to teach a student and what each individual student brings to us in experience. Which, of course, is nearly impossible in a group band or orchestra experience in the elementary, middle, and high school scenarios with very few exceptions. A private instructor is required in almost every scenario.

So, back to breathing. The number one thing a wind teacher should be helping a student with is breathing. Every lesson should begin with a breath study. Working not only on a good tone but a variety of volumes with control and beauty. Since it's at the start of a lesson, the idea has more impact. Someone who is shy should practice noise and someone who is outgoing should work on control.

Group intonation can be helped by getting all members in a section to play the same volume despite the fight that is going on with the students and their equipment. Start with one person. It can be the last person in the section or the first person, it makes no difference. Ask them to play a note. Then ask another person to play a note. Ask the one who is playing soft to play louder and the person who is playing loud to play softer. Do this until the pitch starts coming together.

In some cases, the length of the barrel on a clarinet or where the slides are positioned on a trumpet can make a difference, but the players will show an uncanny way of jumping over this hurdle if they know you are asking them to play in tune.

It may hurt them in the long run to force their instrument to play in a way it's not designed to. Then the schoolteacher or private instructor must intervene and improve the quality of the set-up of the instrument. This should be introduced early on, so students know the importance of their air column and how to manipulate the sound to the advantage of all. One of the things that all professional musicians understand is playing at the relatively same volume as others.

**Building muscles is the same.
no matter what kind you are building—
Physical, Mental, or Emotional**

CHAPTER 2

Teachers, Students, and Learning

*Part of teaching is helping students learn
how to tolerate ambiguity, consider possibilities,
and to ask questions that are unanswerable.*
— Sara Lawrence-Lightfoot

*Where there is clarity, there is no choice.
And where there is choice, there is misery.*
—Peter Tork

Learning music is a lifetime experience. Few, if any of us, master the whole expanse of the music discipline.

Practice one minute a day—or more. This is a rule that cannot be ignored. It is one of the keys to your success. I will remind you of this many times in this book. One-minute turns into more time on the instrument as the student grows.

It is told that the famous classical violinist, Joshua Heifetz, was on tour in the American South, and upon hearing a local country Western fiddler, was heard to say, "That is the greatest violinist I have ever heard." A country fiddler humbled the most famous soloist of his day.

We all teach each other, and we all learn from each other. It's important to be open to knowledge. What I want to write about here is both the formal and informal student/teacher relationships.

First, there are relatively few "good" students and relatively few "good" teachers. It has to do with the 10% rule. The 10% rule says that only 10% in any endeavor really know what they are doing or have a committed interest in a subject. Wonderful news if we must pick a surgeon, isn't it?

With the number of people in this world, 10% of teachers are experts. But in this world of many millions of people, that gives us a big pool for the 10% of the teachers we deem qualified. By the same token, there are a huge number of teachers that fall in the other 90%.

I don't know if that percentage is correct, however, there is no doubt in my mind that there are relatively few great teachers and just as few committed students.

You know what they call the student who placed last in medical school, don't you?

. . . Doctor

Another dilemma we have is that many accomplished musicians of artistic quality should be teaching (at least on a part-time basis) but don't want to. I believe that we all have a duty to pass on our knowledge to honor the teachers who passed the information to us.

While I am decrying the scarcity of quality students and teachers, I must admit that the knowledge and expertise available to us today are better than has been the case at any other time in history. And every generation gets better.

Most of us can turn on the radio or free video 24 hours a day and listen to any style of music. This was not even possible 75 years ago.

Even if we live in a place where the radio choices are not bountiful, today we can listen on the Internet or order CDs and never leave our homes. We can also download music directly from the Internet. This also was not possible 50 or even 30 years ago. There are instructions on videotape, CD-ROM, the Internet, and who knows what's next. This is the greatest Renaissance in the history of humankind. There is no doubt in my mind about that.

The 10% rule has delivered us many experts to forge the way. Ten percent of the experts in our field in this modern world would be a lot of people. *It should be the desire of the student to be in the top 10%, and it should be the desire of the teacher to continue to learn more, on a regular basis, to impart the greatest depth of knowledge possible to the student.*

The informal method of learning is an invaluable one. To be genuinely interested, to ask questions. To be with people "in the know."

I was on a movie date once, with a difficult solo to play. My stand partner leaned over to me and said, "If you think this way, it might be easier." I took his advice. A music lesson for sure.

In almost every case the formal method of teaching is mandatory and is the partner to informal learning. Informal learning is slow and relaxed. Formal learning allows us to measure growth, and teach in a methodical way, thus accelerating learning.

We are, in fact, responsible for our own education.

A teacher's main function is to understand the ego of a student and impart knowledge so the student can best explore the information given. The teacher also functions to keep the student on the most direct learning path. Sometimes this is done with discipline.

It's best when a teacher can command the respect of the student. If that's not possible, the teacher should demand respect. If that's not possible, the teacher should terminate the relationship.

The student must always pay to learn formally. This can be in the form of money, or if the student has limited funds, some exchange with the teacher should be worked out. This concept reinforces the idea that it's "an honor to pay." If a parent is paying for lessons, they should ask the student to pay part of the cost, even if it's only a very small amount. It is best to learn early on that learning costs something. Both teacher and student must constantly remember that, at times, learning can be a painful process.

A good teacher will provide sincere care and nurturing.

There are just a few more things I would like to say directly to the student:

- Let your teacher be your friend, and not your drill sergeant, though occasionally that may be necessary.
- The piano and the voice are the master instruments in Western music. Don't hesitate to sing or play the piano early in your learning curve.

The teacher must be respectful of the inexperience of the student, acknowledge the long journey ahead, and offer encouragement. Periods of rapid growth and development can be followed by confusion, frustration, and even apathy.

In a way, it's like a backburner stew. The ingredients are put in separately according to how long they need to be cooked, and at some future point, those ingredients become stew. As new ingredients are added to the finished stew, it takes time for them to develop into what the new stew will be.

Students and teachers alike should make every attempt to "leave their ego at the door." Enlightened humility should be a part of our discipline. If we don't develop it early on, our music will teach us soon enough.

It's also important to know the difference between real humility and self-deprecation.

We are all where we are today. If we practice, we grow. If we don't practice, our skills diminish. It's best to recognize this fact and be kind to ourselves. What we do is our decision.

While there are many ideas and techniques to be learned on the Internet, and from other sources, a serious student must always have a competent teacher.

REMEMBER:

Be happy with where you are
while you are trying to get where you want to be.

Dear Students:

Never cancel a lesson capriciously.
That is probably the lesson that you need the most.

Sincerely,
A Teacher

There are students whose best hope is just to better understand music, have improved listening skills, and develop a true appreciation of the art of music.

Many students will not excel, due to the time requirement and difficulty of the task. It is the responsibility of the teacher of those students to understand that fact and introduce material that will train the student in music appreciation. It is the duty of the student and their parents to see that the student has a private teacher.

The best way for young students to excel is to have their parents come to sit through the private lesson and then, a few times a week, sit with the student while they study their music. I guess, I never understood why a parent would sit with the student doing their math or reading homework, but don't consider music homework.

Selecting a teacher is an important matter. Young students, by their parent's arrangements, generally select the closest, or perhaps least expensive teacher near their home. It may be the local music store or a teacher on a school district list. Another way is to find an active professional musician to guide the student. I have a video on YouTube entitled "A First Teacher" that will help make that decision. When you are searching for a music instructor in your area, consider what a golf lesson costs. That is a fair price for a music teacher too. Of course, teachers with more knowledge and success charge more—and deserve it.

College students most often *are required* to study with a staff teacher. That does not mean the student cannot get coaching from an additional person if they want. It is the student's choice whether to tell the assigned teacher or not. In many colleges and conservatories, there are many very qualified instructors.

In either instance, the student is "stuck" with the luck of the draw. The student may find a fantastic teacher with whom they can really connect. The odds are, however, that in many cases the student ends up with the wrong teacher.

At a certain age, the student (*sometimes on the advice of a teacher*) must decide and recognize why they enjoy the mental discipline of studying music. Is it a hobby? Is it to be in the school band or orchestra? Is it because they want to get good enough to get into a big College Marching Band? Or is it because they plan to pursue a career in teaching or as a professional musician?

If the student is planning a career as a teacher or as a professional musician, the choice of teachers becomes even more critical.

For those contemplating a career as a professional musician, they should realize that often in their formal study, which includes college and private study, there will be a 5- to 10-year ramping up of those skills on their own and making the necessary contacts to work. That's assuming that they achieve a remarkably high minimum performance standard during their studies. Do we ever quit studying?

There are a couple of things that will make you a success in the music business: How well you play and how many good friends and colleagues you cultivate in the business.

Be in the right place at the right time.

If you are planning to play in a symphony you *must* be a virtuoso on your instrument.

My suggestion to any student seeking a teacher is to take a lesson from several teachers to see which one they develop a rapport with. Or possibly have a Zoom meeting with the teacher. A new teacher should be able to open new vistas to the student in the first few lessons.

If cost is an object in selecting a teacher, it's important to remember that *a lesson every two weeks with the right teacher is better than a lesson every week with the wrong teacher.* Having said that, it's still better to take a lesson every week as it energizes the student to study.

A good teacher can give the student enough to work on in one lesson to last them for many years. The reason to go back to that teacher on a regular basis is that it's impossible for the student to remember all the subtleties that were taught. In addition, this regular study allows the teacher to refine the needs of the student. It also forces the student to prepare for the weekly lesson. Preparation cannot be put off.

Another purpose of regular study is to bring the student back to the path of optimal learning. Any good student who can think on their own will constantly be taking side paths to find their own answers, which is a good thing. The teacher can recognize correct and incorrect tangents the student may be taking and advise the student where a certain path may be folly.

For those students selecting a college, it's best to find out who the private instructor will be, travel to that city, and take a lesson. This could help immeasurably in the selection of a school.

For those students contemplating a career as a professional musician, it's helpful to find a teacher who can be of some assistance professionally, when the student attains mastery of the instrument. The first consideration, however, is naturally the quality of teaching and the teacher's understanding of the subject matter.

If there is a musician that the student admires so much that they want to emulate that person, the student should make every effort to find that person and ask for lessons, even if this is only possible on a part-time basis.

If there is a particular style of music the student wants to learn, they should make every effort to find a teacher who is in that specialty.

We all sound like someone else before we find our own sound. At least most of us.

Doublers are in a special category when searching for a teacher, as they play more than one instrument. Much depends on the specialty the doubler decides on. A doubler that wants to specialize in jazz/pop will want to study with an expert in the improvising field. Perhaps and preferably that teacher doubles too. Someone who is interested in performing in a Broadway pit should study with someone that specializes in that genre. Doubling teachers tend to know the problems of doublers.

Doublers also have a larger overview of music styles because of the many performance circumstances they participate in.

In almost every case, I additionally suggest studying with single-instrument musicians who specialize. Few doublers can teach the subtleties of making an oboe reed like a full-time oboist who spends time every day with reeds. Likewise, few doublers can impart the special knowledge required to produce a "legit" sound on the flute.

Another advantage to a "specialist" teacher is that they know the literature for that instrument.

A jazz teacher will teach the student "tunes" like a flute specialist can introduce the symphonic, concerto, and sonata literature to the student.

Learning is a natural process. We all learn at our own speed. Accelerated learning is most effective when supervised and practiced.

A teacher, a mentor, or a peer can help us by example, with inspiration, motivation, and the discipline necessary for accelerated learning.

Select wisely!

The psychological understanding of people is crucial for a teacher to have a rapport with a student. Every student, as a person, brings many complex combinations of factors and thoughts to a lesson. That includes home life, school life, life experiences, love of music, habits, and even how they came out of the womb. Just look, everyone looks so different! And each person thinks and acts differently too. Even knowing if a student learns by listening and rote, or as a reader of music enters the student/teacher relationship. Introverts and extroverts need to be taught differentlytoo.

The study of psychology is important for a teacher to pursue. Perhaps it's all psychology until the most artistic level of learning. So many teachers simply teach the same way their teachers taught them, like a parent and offspring relationship. That is not enough. Teachers must see the *inner student*. How the student learns, and how the student perceives is important. Does the student have a winner/loser mentality, or do they want to study music for its intrinsic value? They may even see fame as a reason to study. Whatever is in a student's concept is important for the teacher to understand, to help facilitate the best learning possible. The psychology of a 9-year-old student might differ from the same student when they are 20. The psychological study of people and learning music is a lifelong study. So, I invite teachers to formally study psychology, as well as music, to be the best teacher they can be.

Just a thought on the very advanced student who knows part of the literature and wants to be a soloist: They should be the student who is at the final step of the assisted study. They are undoubtedly studying from a very advanced teacher and a teacher that is most likely a virtuoso.

I feel that the advanced student should never be told how to play. Instead of telling the student how and why to play a phrase, the student should be *asked why they played the music in question the way they did*. Ask the student to tell what they are thinking about in a particular phrase. Then offer them an option to play it another way, probably the way the teacher would play it.

The teacher might suggest something for the student to listen to that shows another way of playing by listening to a recording of some sort. Or the teacher can play the phrase the way they think it should be played. If the student doesn't accept the teacher's suggestion, let the student do it their own way. If the student does not accept the teacher's suggestion enough times, they may no longer need a teacher. Or depending on the teacher's experience, the student could be advised to try another teacher.

Just one last thing that Noa Kagayama, who has a weekly blog, reminded me of: We all have negative thoughts about ourselves for one reason or another. It might be something someone said to us that was critical, or it might be a disappointment that only we know about. The idea is that each time we have a negative assessment of ourselves, we must first recognize it, then confront it. If it is true, it is in the past—so forgive yourself and look forward. If it is not true, recognize the fact and move on. The thoughts may come up again. Dismiss them again. The future is where we are going, not the past. Don't keep doing the negative thing that's bothering you.

In review, let me say that the student/teacher relationship is the most important music relationship we are likely to have.

The main thing a teacher can teach a student is: Concept

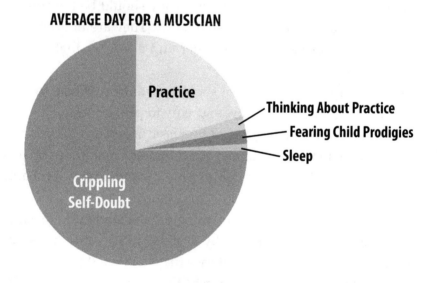

AVERAGE DAY FOR A MUSICIAN

FOR STUDENTS

Having said some of these things earlier in this chapter, I would like to speak directly to the student. This whole student and teacher relationship can be summed up in one sentence for the student:

*"A student owes it to the teacher to study their
lessons in earnest almost every day."*

In a great music lesson, the teacher presents information and then asks for feedback from the student to make sure they understand what was said.

Nobody likes to be told what to do. That's almost always true.

Students want to have lessons they share with their teacher. The question is how experienced you are as a student what the teacher can share with you and what must simply be taught. The student should never fear asking a question when they don't understand something, even if it's not part of a particular lesson. Interaction is best for both the teacher and the student.

And please, never hesitate to write on your music. It serves as a reminder of a note or passage that must be practiced or can be a reminder of an accidental or some other marking.

As a student at any level, you have a lot on your mind. It's good to have something as intense as music and its study so your mind can be totally occupied by something important. The ruminations about non-important subjects, like who said what to whom that you may be carrying with you are set aside. Practice, playing, or studying allows your mind to concentrate on a single subject. The secret is to be positive in your approach and realize that music is a long road that never comes to an end. There is no reason to rush learning. It will happen in the time it's meant to, if you play almost every day.

Pick some time every day, every week, every month, and every year to take a brief rest from all you have on your mind. That's when the real learning takes place. It's called digestion. You give yourself time to think about what you've learned and what adjustments will be required. The yearly break should be a week or more. Think about your music and relax in a beautiful place. You will find that when you come back to practice, your hands and your brain will be a bit off-kilter, but your chops will come back quickly.

Students are all at very different levels, and you need to understand that. Assuming a beginning student is young, the parents can help a lot. You should ask them to attend your lessons, tape the lessons, and be there to help you when there is something you don't understand while practicing. A videotape will help them help you too.

Don't kid yourself. You must remember that your teacher was once a student. As teachers, we have tried all the "tricks" to make *our* teachers think we practiced the whole week. So, make no mistake, your teacher most likely knows how much you practiced in a week's time almost down to the minute. However, how long you practice is not as important as playing your instrument every day.

Again, as I said to you, start by practicing a minute a day. If you miss a days' practice, remember that *consistent practice is the key to progress*. Also remember, it's a long road to mastering an instrument and you aren't going to learn faster than the river is flowing, so patience and persistence are always in order in your playing days. The beginner may be befuddled just putting the instrument together and playing three or four notes. In the beginning, one minute of practice is likely to turn out to be five or ten minutes if your body holds up to it. As your playing improves, your practice time should increase. After a couple of years, if you aren't getting at least one minute in per day, perhaps you would be a better listener than a musician. Or perhaps you should try another teacher.

As you advance, look for other ensembles to play with besides your school band or orchestra. The more you study music, the more opportunities will come your way. If you know you only want to play a certain type of music, that makes it easier for you, as you may only have to find one group outside of school to play with. Your private teacher (and everyone should have a private teacher) can help you find other groups to play with. Granted that is more difficult if you live in a rural area where you must drive a long way to play with others, but in or near bigger cities, this should be fairly easy.

Remember there are always musicians better than you and some not as proficient. Respect all players that are trying their best. It's better to keep mute about other people's playing unless they ask your opinion. If you have something that can help them, be kind in your manner of helping them when asked.

Until you get to the international soloist position, the best thing to aim to do is not necessarily to be the best, but to be *one of the best*. If you happen to be the best, it will be noticed without you having to prove the fact. We occasionally learn more from our friends and experiences than from our private teachers.

Try playing for others even in your early years—your family, your relatives, your neighbors, or anyone else who will listen to you. If you are not good, at least you will be cute, and everyone will enjoy your performance. Remember that most people don't understand the difficulty of music, so if someone says something negative about your playing, take it with a grain of salt and decide for yourself if there was any validity to what they had to say. If you agree with them, fix it. If need be, ask your teacher during a lesson.

As a student, you may think you don't have enough time to get to your music every day.

We always make time for what we really want to do.

Practice is not a team sport. The difference between a group in music and in sports is if you can't make it to a rehearsal or performance there is likely nobody to replace you. In sports, there is usually a line of other athletes ready and trained to go into the game. In music, if you don't do your share for the success of a group, there is a hole where you normally sit. There are no substitutions. Musicians are playing varsity at every point in their careers.

That makes your intentions and learning your instrument very important.

When you practice, take your instrument out, make any adjustments needed to play. Do that, and then just sit for about 30 to 60 seconds and breathe deeply in and out slowly. Now you are ready for your first note of the day. The first note you play is the most important note you play. It could be the first note of the day, or it could be a solo part when playing in an ensemble. People hear your first note more clearly than subsequent notes. Make the first note a beauty.

I talk about music being a solitary act. But think about it. When in most of your days do you have time to sit down and have time for yourself? Completely to yourself. No one telling you what to do. To practice, to think about what you have practiced, and to understand what you have practiced can be a satisfying time alone.

Like all things, there is balance in music. So, you might be playing very well and then you come upon hard times when the instrument feels funny, you aren't making the progress you are used to, and what was easy becomes difficult. The cure for this is patience. You have just reached a plateau—a place where all the learning you've done is being gestated. All those ingredients you cut up and put in a pot are becoming stew. Enjoy that. Soon the routine will begin its journey again . . . until the next plateau. There is no rhyme or reason when these plateaus happen, but you will notice them.

One of the things you want to do on these plateaus is to make sure your instrument is in good working order. We have the impulse to blame ourselves or the instrument. So that we don't go crazy, it's best just to get the instrument looked at by your repairperson to give you some peace of mind.

I tend to have my instruments looked at whenever there is a big change in weather, especially humidity changes. If you were taught how to clean your instrument, it's a good time to do that before you take it to your repairperson.

Another tip is to always have the best instrument you can afford. Also, become acquainted with all the aftermarket equipment for your instrument. Keep trying every new gadget that comes along, and please only buy the one you like. Don't listen to anyone else regarding these trials, except perhaps your teacher.

Don't forget to listen, but don't listen to just music. Listen to everything and everybody. Hold back your opinion until you have researched a subject and have the facts in your mind, and not just opinions. You watch, you listen, and you make decisions based on your best-studied insights.

For the intermediate and advanced student, whenever you are learning a new piece of solo literature or orchestra music, find as many recordings of the piece as you can. You will notice if you are listening closely, that most interpretations of what you are studying are much different from recording to recording. This means to me that we are allowed a more relaxed idea of interpretation, and not necessarily one that is insisted upon by a teacher. And, of course, if there is a live performance of the piece near you, be sure to go and hear it—and see and hear how the audience reacts.

The more mature you get, and the more technique you attain, the more you should start making your own decisions.

There are those of you who may not be yet ready to make your own decisions about your studies. If you are strong-minded, you may practice in your own manner and see how it goes. That's okay. However, if you listen to your teacher and take lessons on a regular basis, your improvement will be much quicker. When you stray from the fastest learning curve, your teacher can bring you back and show you the possible folly of your ways.

Learn the stories attached to the music. Read about composers and the times they lived in. Learn the stories about unique events that happen when rehearsing and performing.

Also, as you get more proficient, learn to read a score. Knowing your own part in a piece of music is good, but knowing every line of a score is superior knowledge in music.

One thing that I feel is important is to learn the piano at least to the point where you can play chords and melodies. Also please let your teachers help you to sing, no matter how bad you think you sound or what fears you harbor.

There are just a few more things I would like to say directly to the student.

Let your teacher be your friend, and not your drill sergeant, though occasionally a drill sergeant may be necessary.

Go to every scheduled private lesson unless you have an extreme emergency. Students tend not to go to a lesson when they are not prepared. That's exactly when you need a lesson the most. There is always something to work on in a lesson, whether it's what you prepared or didn't prepare. Like practicing, taking a lesson on a very regular basis is one of the keys to success. Don't depend on the Internet to be your primary teacher. Use the Internet only as an adjunct to your teacher.

The piano and the voice are the master instruments in Western music. Don't hesitate to sing or play the piano early in your learning curve.

Learn to play chords and melodies on the piano, and learn to sing, as the art of music is in singing on your instrument.

CHAPTER 3

The Physical Technique
The Body, and Health

HEALTH

The body carries out the orders of the mind. So, how important is the body? Ponder long and hard on that question. What are you going to do about it?

A weakened body will tax the ability of the mind to react clearly. How important is that? It takes a lot of extra energy for the mind to work with pain and physical distraction present.

Wilfred Kujalla, who had an unprecedented 48-year career and retired at age 76 from his principal piccolo position with the Chicago Symphony, was asked about his secret of longevity with that orchestra. His answer: "GOOD HEALTH."

The body slowly weakens with age. To keep our skills for as long as possible, it's best to deal with this fact as young as possible. Each and every major injury throughout our life will revisit us as we age.

The body keeps the score.

My retired friend and I were talking one day and he said, "My wife and I practice every day, so we get worse slower." I do the same. If you really love music and it's not just a job for you, you will play as long as your body lets you.

So, my suggestion is to find exercise and play; that you can continue to practice or modify it as you age.

In short, take care of yourself! You will be able to play music and work longer with ease.

> **Be thankful for what you already have.**

POSTURE

If we practice a posture as "correct," we tend to defend that posture in our own minds *and thus lock ourselves to that mode of playing*. There are, however, certain basic postures that we should practice as an ideal to be varied upon.

Look at your favorite musician, someone who plays the same instrument and the same style as you do. One of the reasons that a person sounds like they do is what their posture—and concept—bring to their approach.

A curved neck, a jaw jutted out, the finger position, and even a tight little toe can influence our sound. Erectness affects the flow of the air and the effect the solar plexus has on our sound.

Every subtle combination of tension and relaxation throughout our whole body makes us sound like we do.

For me, that approach has always been the middle ground. Not too tight, not too loose. Not with the instrument fully extended and not with the instrument too close to the body.

I believe that if one can attain this balance of the physical approach, the movement to the more extreme approaches when required, becomes more plausible.

Except for improvisation, which is a different subject, I believe this is why so few musicians can master the transition from symphonic style to popular music.

In each case, the concept taught or accepted has locked the body into an "ideal" that should not be violated (in our own mind). While useful to lock into an "ideal" to perform a certain type of music, it seems silly that one would have to live monogamously with that one way of playing and even in some cases, defend it as the only way to play.

Just do me a favor. Once. Every time you practice. Do something physically different.

For those of you tight players, slouch and practice a minute of noise. For those of you loose musicians, be very erect and proper and play a nice, controlled *medium loud* long tone—and feel your body.

The easiest way to play, of course, is when the body is not fighting itself. That is, when the muscles aren't fighting each other. *That is relaxed!*

We must remember that long tones (a single note held for 15 seconds or more) are the best time to study the body.

Long tones are the Zen meditation (or prayers if you prefer) of the musician. To be mentally quiet with our internal dialogue turned down or preferably off, and to feel each and every part of the body, and how it affects our own personal sound, is the goal.

Long tones should be a daily component of our practice schedule; not just a warm-up for the barrage of notes to come, but instead, centering ourselves for the withdrawal from the mundane and busy thoughts of the day. It's a study of the physical and how it affects all that we do with the instrument in our hands. Limit long tones to 3 to 5 minutes of a daily practice schedule unless there is something you are trying to cure. However, do it every time you play.

The middle ground allows you to change directions with less work.

Remember, when you are breathing to use your back to accept air from the lungs and try to not lift your shoulders while inhaling.

There are certain physical rules that are irrefutable, as far as my experience goes.

The number one rule? *Keep the fingers rounded.* For example, it's imperative that the fingers are round and relaxed when playing. The feeling is like the arms are hanging down to our side completely relaxed. When the arm is raised to the instrument the fingers don't "flex" to finger a note. If the fingers need to flex tighter or move in an unnatural way to finger a note, have an expert modify your instrument to fit your hand. In most instances that's not the case. Usually, the reality is that the musician can, with some study, adjust to a natural approach to holding the instrument. This is something that can be practiced while not blowing through your instrument too.

Many instrumentalists flatten the fingernail joint of their finger (hyper-extended) when depressing a key. The result is a disastrous four movements each time the key is depressed. Depress the key, then depress the joint. That is two movements. Lift the joint, then lift the finger, that is another two movements, for a grand total of four movements of the finger for each note. Twice the work for just one note.

For most instruments, a rounded finger pressing and releasing from the fingernail are two movements. It seems obvious that if we can eliminate the extra two movements, we have the potential to play twice as fast, or twice as easily.

A simple physical exercise is to study the movements of just going from one note to the next. How do the fingers function, look, and feel? Practice just two isolated notes to find out. Do this exercise every time you find difficulty going from one note to another. For the beginner, this study will save hours of frustration on wasted practice time. For the advanced musician who has not yet realized the folly of wasted motion, this drill should be quite a freeing experience.

Another example of getting rid of tension for my flutist friends is simply turning the torso slightly over your left leg. If you aren't doing this already you will immediately feel the release of tension throughout the top half of the body.

On flute, we want the bottom of the chair parallel to the chin and parallel to the ground, so the airway stays open. If standing, the chin is still parallel to the ground. I have found when standing it's helpful to have the left foot a little in front of the right foot.

Practice both positions, sitting, and standing, every time you practice. Get used to being comfortable both ways.

The short answer is to pay attention to the body daily.

Finger/Tone Exercises
The Chromatic Scale
Is the Alphabet of Music!

I have found that the chromatic exercise of five notes repeated three times with a long tone is an excellent method to study the movements of the body and focus on the correct support of the long tone. Notice that the place to breathe is after the first note or the top note. This is especially important when playing to slowly breathe at these points, as when we start to run out of air, in an attempt to save our lives, the body tends not to work as well, if at all.

You can find my video of this on YouTube. It's titled "The Chromatic Scale." (*See below.*)

EXAMPLE 1.

3 x's

Study this chromatic exercise starting on every note. Begin the exercise by starting on any note, the lowest note of the instrument if you can, or the note "C" and go up chromatically. After that progression is comfortable, practice the exercise around the circle of 5ths.

There are other variations of chromatic exercise and, in fact, you can devise your own exercises based on any combination of notes, chromatic or not.

The chromatic exercise is a valuable tool to revisit throughout our playing careers. I have been using it as my warm-up, and to fix finger problems when I get lazy, for 50+ years.

The chromatic scale is the alphabet of music. Learn it as well as you know the alphabet of words.

Another similar chromatic exercise you can work on after Exercise #1, is the *Flight of the Bumblebee,* herein known as Chromatic Exercise #2. (*See below.*)

EXAMPLE 2

It's important to note in both exercises that not every exercise will be the same difficulty due to the fingerings involved. The ultimate goal is to play these fast. However, the *immediate* goal is to play the exercise on each note, to study the fingers to allow faster playing. So, each exercise is likely to be at a different speed for many years. When all the exercises are about the same speed as Exercise #1 and the long tone is solid, you can go on to number #2. This can likely take years unless you really work on it every day.

The purpose of the long tone is to learn to listen to the note you are playing and to hold it without a quiver. It's also a good time to study your body and discern what is relaxed and what is tight.

SUPPORT

This brings us to probably the most misunderstood and abstract concept in the physical production of sound: **Support.**

I wonder if support can be taught. It's such an internal feeling. Each physical body will feel something a little different.

A person 6' 7" will certainly feel something different than a person who is 5' 4". The overall physical posture of the musician will also play into the inner focus of support.

Is it tight? Is it loose? Does it come from high in the torso? Does it come from low in the abdomen? Where to supply the support? What muscles are used to provide the support? What is the diaphragm? What does it do? The questions just go on and on as do the theories to define this abstract concept.

My suggestions for support are:

1. Breathe in unencumbered, fill the front and back of your lungs.

2. Blow out unencumbered

3. Only utilize as much air as you need for the job.

4. Only tighten the abdomen enough for each particular task, the amount of support will change with the situation.

5. Apply the support so the solar plexus is not tightened, because this also tightens the throat. That equates to supporting low in the torso and storing some air in the back.

   Try this exercise: Tighten the solar plexus with its surrounding muscles as tight as you can. I mean really tight. Now feel the tightness in the throat. That's the feeling we always try to avoid.

6. Use the ears (listen to yourself) and the concept (listen to others) to control the ever-changing support to create each subtlety of tone.

The muscles of the throat should be generally relaxed and the airway malleable and open.

Avoid tightening your throat.

THE TONGUE

When not in use, the tongue should be totally relaxed and flaccid at the bottom of the mouth. This is true when blowing, unless the tongue is being used to color the tone. For flutists, when tonguing, as soon as you make contact with the roof of your mouth, immediately return the tongue to the bottom of your mouth. Do not tongue through the teeth or mouth. Tu, Du, or some other sound is good for training the tongue to touch the roof of the mouth for flutists.

For reed instrumentalists, you must choose which part of the reed you are going to touch when tonguing, and how hard you will depress the cane. After tonguing, like the flute, your tongue will go to the bottom of your mouth to wait to be used again. Please do not tongue between the reed and the mouthpiece, or for double reed players, in between the two blades of the cane. Like the flute, thinking of Tu or Du while touching the reed is helpful. Many times, starting a note is called an *attack*. But in tonguing, please don't attack the note. Instead, think of the reed or the roof you your mouth as a hot plate, so immediately after tonguing the note, the tongue is in a hurry to get back to the bottom of your mouth. Tongue the reed as is appropriate to the music you are playing, lightly for soft passages and more aggressively for loud or raucous music.

Keep in mind that a symphonic musician and a Rock and Roll musician will be using a different part of the tongue and reed to create their attack, due to style and volume.

A common problem is that the back of the tongue being raised on a regular basis impacts the airway and locks the tone in a negative way.

THE MOUTH

The mouth and the muscles that control the jaw, like all other aspects of the airway, should be as relaxed as possible, and still be able to form the *embouchure* (use of face muscles) and do the work at hand.

For flutists, the mouth controls the opening between the top and bottom teeth, thus altering the airflow to the embouchure and, in fact, influencing the free flow of air into the flute. While creating the embouchure, be sure to leave room between the top and bottom teeth to allow the air to exit.

For the double-reed instrumentalists, in addition to the embouchure and airflow delivery, the mouth and teeth help to determine the opening of the reed aperture and vibration of the reed. Biting will cause fatigue (as does most everything). Both single- and double-reed musicians should think of the embouchure with equal pressure coming from all sides of the mouth, not just the top and bottom, but like a rubber band.

For the single-reed musician, the manner and concept of how the teeth are positioned on the top of the mouthpiece are critical to sound production. The position of the lower jaw and its muscles are extremely important in relation to the top teeth. That alignment can create, in the worst-case scenario, muscle soreness and TMJ, or in the best-case scenario, a flexible cushion for tone production.

As with so many other studies, the study of the airway and its components are best accomplished with long tones.

THE EMBOUCHURE

The embouchure, composed of the lips and the muscles that control the lips and the jaw, is an important contact between the body and the instrument. Some people even use the muscles in their forehead as part of their embouchure. We should try to only use facial muscles whenever possible. Flexing the forehead creates tension, so best to try and avoid that.

From my point of view, we may safely say all the muscles in the head and throat add to the definition of the embouchure since they all influence the tone in some way.

The best example of this is the furrowed eyebrow and forehead. Relax the third eye and the forehead, and the color and spirit of the tone will change.

The concepts and teaching of the embouchure are varied, and I will leave that to the many pundits on the subject.

My take and contribution to the subject are only that the more we can use the corners of the mouth to control the embouchure, the more suppleness we will have in the lips to control the tone.

A thought for the single-reed musicians is that the feeling should be more like a rubber band encircling the mouthpiece with pressure coming from all sides of the mouth.

INSTRUMENT POSITION

The angle of the instrument is important for tone production and intonation and is an extension of the general concept of playing.

The angle of the instrument for double-reed and single-reed musicians cannot be precisely determined. Much has to do with the style being played, the size of the musician and instrument, and the effect the angle has on the sound and intonation of each separate individual. In general, I would say again that having the instrument too close to the body or too far away from the body is not generally a desired daily habit.

I find it best to experiment with extremes. Hold the instrument way too high, then hold it close to the body, and then halfway in between. What are the tonal and pitch ramifications for you?

I always tend to select the middle position, as it allows me to go in either direction to affect sound and pitch more easily when required.

For the flute, my idea of body/instrument position is a little more rigid. Why? Because the instrument is not placed in the mouth, there are many more physical variables to be manipulated.

If we as flutists can limit our set-ups to basic angles, we have a basis to make slight changes that will positively affect our performance.

My idea of the basic flute set-up is:

1. Torso 45 degrees to the left of the left leg.

2. Flute parallel to the ground with the keys facing straight up.

3. Bottom of chin parallel to the ground.

4. Hole of the blow plate parallel to the ground (i.e., is in line with the center of the keys).

5. The torso should be bent slightly forward from the waist, so the body takes a physically superior position to the instrument. As you bend slightly forward don't roll the flute toward your lips.

6. Shoulders should be relaxed and elbows down with a straight right wrist and curved fingers. The thumb of the right hand is under the finger that it naturally falls under when the arms are down at the side.

7. Left hand flopped back and cradling the flute (i.e., the flute is "sitting" on the first joint of the first finger of the left hand).

Once we know we can get into this basic "mathematical" setup of the body and the instrument, we can have a fair amount of confidence in a basic position and control of the myriad of position variables that each movement of our body creates. And most importantly, it becomes repeatable. It does require diligence and attention to assume this position when sitting in a variety of chairs and physical situations, as well as standing.

Variations of this basic position can be made to suit the body of the individual and any physical constriction they may have. You should be reminded, however, that we can work from this basic position no matter what size we are.

REVIEW

In review, studying the physical elements of playing long tones, the chromatic exercises are best. The chromatic exercise allows you to keep your fingers loose, with the long tone allowing you to practice separation of the air and the body. In other words, as you play louder don't let your fingers and body tighten. In fact, try and let them be looser.

Practice extremes of tightness and looseness to find out the middle ground or the correct amount of tension for your individual tone production, style, and ease of technique.

Learning music is a lifetime experience. Few, if any of us, master the whole expanse of the discipline.

If you want something you've never had,
you must be willing to do something you've never done.
—Thomas Jefferson

CHAPTER 5

Equipment

Unless we are incredibly lucky and have an exceptional instrument put in our hands early on, we all tend to be on a constant search for equipment that will make our tasks easier.

The better a musician becomes, the more they understand their own equipment needs. A classic example is oboe reeds. We can't make a better oboe reed for ourselves until we can play the oboe better, so we can know what we want the reed to do. Every time we get better, we can make better reeds. This is a continual cycle.

The same is true of a single reed, a single-reed mouthpiece, and even a flute headjoint. The more subtlety we develop in our playing, the more subtlety we expect out of our equipment.

We also need equipment that makes our style of playing easier. One would not easily perform with a closed mouthpiece that may be perfect in a classical situation, in a big loud jazz band, or in a rock and roll situation. So, the equipment must match the job at hand.

Equipment is a special concern for the freelance musician. When called for a recording session, a doubler may not know what style is required that day. As woodwind players, we are often called for "solo" positions, as opposed to, say, a "section violinist."

I regularly brought three mouthpieces for the saxophone to every job: one for classical, one for middle-of-the-road playing, and one that can play loud and edgy. It doesn't hurt to have a couple of clarinet mouthpieces either.

I have known oboists to come to the job with both a rosewood *and* a grenadilla instrument because of the tone color differences. Many piccolo players bring a wood *and* a silver piccolo to the job. It's important to be ready to play a solo at any moment on a great instrument. The great instrument will help bring your solo to life.

A set-up that worked in a wet-sounding concert hall may not work in a dry-sounding pit with baffles, carpets, and foam on the walls. So, we must also know where we will be working. Symphonic musicians that work in mostly the same auditorium and sit in the same place for every concert have an advantage. I have even known musicians who will point their instruments to a certain place in the hall as they get the best feedback on sound from that position.

An instrument is very personal and an extension of the musician. The feel, the physical weight, the response, the spring tension, and other elements of an instrument combine in creating a comfort level for the player.

Every professional musician who plays a single-reed instrument that I know has a minimum of one shoebox full of old mouthpieces. Most have many more. Most advanced flutists have several flutes and several headjoints. Again, as we improve, we have a better idea of what equipment we need to do our job better.

Occasionally, we try an instrument that feels great immediately. While first impressions can be valid, it's still important to investigate further, as one would do with all instrument purchases.

Sometimes we like an instrument on impulse, just because it's different from the one that we are currently playing. Sometimes, we are fooled, because it sounds freer or more covered than what we are currently playing on. Or sometimes we are fooled, just because the instrument plays louder than what we are currently playing on.

SOME TESTS

Always run an instrument through the "tests" before purchasing.

1. Mechanical Condition: Check to make sure the pads are covering well and are not sticky. If in doubt about the repairability of an instrument, take it to your repairperson.

2. Intonation: With a mechanical tuner, check all the intervals starting on different notes. Do this test without adjusting to make any notes purposely play in tune. While each interval doesn't need to tune "dead center," it should be close enough to reach the pitch with minimal adjustment when performing.

3. A/B the new instrument with the one you are currently using. Also, record both instruments, if possible, so you can listen while not playing.

4. Have someone else play both instruments randomly. This is best if you can keep your eyes closed while the other person plays so you don't listen with prejudice. Listen from several different distances, and in different acoustic situations.

5. Try some difficult finger combinations to make sure the instrument keywork feels good and can facilitate those different passages.

Test the instrument slowly. It's only necessary to blast a couple of barrages of notes to make sure the instrument plays fast enough. Listen to basic tone, evenness of tone, and intonation.

After you feel that the instrument is right for you, see if it can be taken on approval, to test in a performance or rehearsal situation with other musicians.

If there is not an urgent need to buy the instrument immediately, "sleep on it" for a night, and go back and try the instrument again. You may also want to play as many other instruments as possible that may be available before you purchase.

It's always easier to buy an instrument than sell it, unless you are a born horn trader at heart. Don't buy impulsively!

Stock instruments (i.e., instruments off the shelf) and stock mouthpieces seldom fit our needs exactly. If they do, we are ahead of the game. If they don't, it's important to have them customized.

A good acoustician that is also a good horn smasher *(repairperson)* is an asset.

As we get to know our instruments intimately, we invariably find notes that we would like to improve the tone, color, or pitch. The acoustician and repairperson can help refine the instrument to our specifications or advise us on the correct actions to be taken.

Likewise, a custom mouthpiece or headjoint can improve and alter the response of an instrument. Tone color, pitch, and the playing character are important facets of any new instrument we purchase.

I like my mouthpiece to work with a reed right out of the box. Most mouthpieces require the reed either to be sanded or clipped a bit. This just adds to the amount of time you must futz with the reed/mouthpiece combination.

When trying a new mouthpiece, in addition to your "good" reed that you take to your mouthpiece maker, take along 3 or 4 reeds that are the best ones out of a couple of boxes, so you have several reeds to try.

REEDS

Did I say somewhere else in this treatise that nothing is perfect? Well, put reeds at the top of the list.

You won't always have a great reed, so just accept the fact, and play on the best one that you have.

Reeds are alive with two life cycles: the first is the growing cycle and the drying process *(cane is greenish when it's cut, and it must lie outside in the sun to get its golden color)*. And the second cycle is when you receive the reed and start to adjust it. The reed is still alive.

There are many things that affect your reed. Was it grown on the sun side, the shady side, the windy side, or the rainy side? All these elements affect each individual reed.

How big are the veins of the reed—in other words, the density of the reed? Suck on the bottom side of the reed and feel the air coming through. This is one of the things you want to fix early on.

The way to make a reed last a long time is to start with the raw reed, ever so lightly sand it, and with a file, close off the holes at the bottom. Then rub the reed for a while. You may want to put some grease from the side of your nose or behind your ear to help seal up the veins. Some people have even been known to rub their reeds with dirt. I don't know if that's necessary, but you might try it and see if it works for you. Balance the reed so both sides respond the same when testing lightly with your fingers and notice how far down each side of the reed flexes. Those are just a few of the fixes.

You must become an expert at adjusting reeds and pairing them with your mouthpiece and ligature. That's the sound-creating marriage that cannot be ignored.

There are some exceptionally good books on reeds available, so I will leave the reader to search them out. Those books will give you sources to find all the tools and measuring devices that are needed to adjust a reed. Of course, a teacher can help too.

I have found the ATG Reed System by Tom Ridenour extremely helpful. Having been a double-reed player for 50 years, I tend to use just a knife and sandpaper. If you do buy his system, I strongly advise you to purchase the video also. To see Tom adjusting a reed blind-folded is quite a pleasure and highly informative. However, there are many reed systems and tools available, and you should be familiar with all of them.

I will suggest that you have a great knife to work with and that you always keep it appropriately sharp. The sharpness that a single-reed musician is looking for is different than a double-reed musician. The sharpness of a single reed knife should be duller so as not to gouge the reed while adjusting it. It's also mandatory to have a good bright light to work in. The sun is the best light source of all, of course. So if you can place your reed table near a window, all the better.

To have good reeds takes time unless we get lucky. It's worth spending the time to have several reeds that always work well and in all situations.

Reed companies come closer than you think in providing you with good products. However, they don't know who you are or how you play, so you *must* learn how to adjust/finish reeds. You will also most likely find a brand of reed that you like the response of. The brand you select might change from season to season, as companies that buy cane and don't have their own reed farms might not get the cane you are looking for. The reeds I like are golden colored and when first put in the mouth taste sweet.

There are good cane years just as there are good wine years. So, when you find a brand of reed you like, and after you have tried a couple of boxes, hoard as many boxes of that lot as you can afford.

Every reed brand is cut differently at each factory, so it's important that you know the style of reed that will work best for you.

Keep in mind that a reed is a living thing. It changes with the humidity. Part of learning to work on a reed includes minimizing how weather affects it. Open pores on a reed are not our friend. The environment you are playing in also determines how you are going to make your reed.

A hard reed plays sharper than a soft reed. It has to do with how much harder the reed requires you to work. Try this. Take your tuner out and play a very soft reed on a long tone and see where it registers. Then do the same thing with a good playing hard reed.

A very good symphonic clarinetist once said, "Play the softest reed you can to do the job that is required."

Also, remember to work on your reeds in a lot of light, sunlight being the best, and you must use a magnifying glass or glasses if the reed is not very clear to you. You must see the reed on which you are working. This is imperative.

I had an interesting experience. One day I was working in a church and suddenly all the reeds I had made at home were not working. Following that, I had a session and the same reeds were working great. The next day I went to a friend's house to play for fun and the reeds didn't want to work again. I came to realize that both the church and my friend's house had a fan close to me. The fan was drying the cane in my mouth as I was playing it. We learn something new every day.

Another idea is to keep the reeds in a leak-proof jar with half mouthwash and half water. Keep them there all the time. The reed will be completely wet every time you take it out. I am still trying this idea out and I will leave it to you to try the same thing for yourself. The mouthwash is to keep the reed from getting mold on it. I have several friends that do this. They don't adjust the reed until it has been sitting in the water overnight. Myself, I prefer

Make sure your reed is completely wet.

to put my reeds in the mouthwash and water solution for about five minutes before I play them on the job or practice, and before adjusting them.

LIGATURES

The ligature brings the reed and mouthpiece to life. It is much more than just a mechanism to hold the reed on.

Like an instrument, if we try ten ligatures of the same brand, one will stand out as superior. The musicians I know have a box laying around with those used ligatures.

Try every ligature around that fits your mouthpiece. When an innovative design comes out, take the time to try it too. Science and the advent of new materials have really increased the number of available ligatures.

Whenever we change mouthpieces, or just on occasion, we should go through our ligatures. As we mature, what we look for in a ligature changes. There is sometimes a gem in our own arsenal waiting to be rediscovered.

There was a man who tried several ligatures, and they all sounded the same. This leads me to believe that the ligature changes the feeling in the mouth of the musician rather than the sound, thus making it more comfortable and better fitting with the mouthpiece, reed, and ligature marriage.

SET-UP

The reed, mouthpiece, and ligature (the set-up) work in conjunction with each other, and with a balance. Change one element and the balance changes.

The reed, of course, changes most often and does not usually require a change of mouthpiece or ligature. Occasionally it does happen though, especially when combined with playing in a different acoustical situation, or when the reed is very bright or dull and requires a change in ligature (and occasionally mouthpiece).

As discussed earlier, ligatures should be reconsidered whenever changing a mouthpiece on a permanent basis.

The fact that the set-up is the sound-generating mechanism as well as the comfort-generating system determines its importance and selection.

For the flutist, the set-up is the headjoint and for the oboist, the reed, staple, and scrape are ever so important. Also, be careful not to wrap the reed above the staple on the double reeds.

It's to our advantage that we stay vigilant about our setup. It's also important to keep in mind your playing situation. A person in a symphony or playing in a chamber music group is not going to be looking for the same equipment as the person playing into a microphone in a Rock and Roll band.

CHAPTER 6

Fear

Fear for musicians is related to several different scenarios.

A fear that can be cured comparatively easily is the fear created by not being prepared. Sounds simple, doesn't it? Just practice a little before the rehearsal or concert and we will "get through it." Unfortunately, that is not the case. Rarely does short-term practicing cure this type of fear.

We have heard the phrase "still waters run deep." That is true of preparedness too. The musician must intrinsically know they are prepared beyond a reasonable doubt. That is a much better level of confidence, which is only made possible by consistent and regular practice.

If learning a piece of music, 100% is the goal. Learn it 200% and you will worry much less.

PREPAREDNESS + OPPORTUNITY = SUCCESS

We must feel confident that even if our internal dialogue completely takes our concentration away, the music will still be played.

Most of us have some level of internal dialogue (i.e., we talk to ourselves). When we are not prepared, the level of internal dialogue increases. As it increases, the possibility of mistakes becomes greater, because the internal dialogue interrupts our concentration. Even more reason to have the music "under our fingers" and beyond the "thinking" level.

> *One of the best lessons you can learn in life,*
> *is to master how to remain calm.*
> **—Catherine Pulsifer**

The goal, of course, is to have little or no internal dialogue and only "react" to the music. Become one with the music!

> *Me vs. Me has been my biggest fight.*
> **—Sanga Noona**

We must realize that preparedness and perfection are two different entities.

We aim for perfection. Unfortunately, few things in this world, including ourselves, are perfect.

Musicians tend to be perfectionists. We usually strive to be perfect. We like the journey, we like solving the puzzles of music, and we understand the beauty of the perfection that we can achieve in our playing.

Let me help put perfection in perspective. A batter in baseball hitting .500 might be considered perfect for the task that they perform. A pitcher, if lucky, will occasionally, in his whole career pitch a "perfect game."

Most musicians expect a .999+ batting average for themselves. While this is attainable with practice, it's still not perfect. It's a dilemma we need to learn to live with.

Anything close to technical perfection still does not include any kind of aesthetic perfection or guarantee that we will feel mentally or physically comfortable while performing. A double dilemma.

In short, while we strive for perfection through preparedness, we must humbly and happily accept the outcome of our hard work, and constantly remind ourselves that perfection is fleeting. The concert is the time to let the preparedness do its job. Now, as always, it's time to perform for serious fun.

Another type of fear, which is cured by repetition, is the fear of facing a new circumstance or playing situation.

A studio musician or pit musician asked to perform "onstage" with some solos to be played can find themselves very disconcerted because they will be featured in front of an audience and viewed as they do their work. These musicians are used to performing in front of their peers that know what they do and appreciate their accomplishments. The inexperience of performing in front of strangers can be quite daunting until they become used to the situation.

For the same reason, I have seen many public performers panic when they knew the music was going to be recorded and listened to over and over and perhaps even be put under the "microscope" of the control room.

How about a musician who has settled on being second chair, having to play first and be in the unwanted spotlight?

Proximity also enters the mix. If one is used to performing with an audience fairly far away, as in a formal concert situation, playing a recital, or in a club where the audience is very close to the performer can be disconcerting.

Again, for the same reason, performers who are used to being close to their audiences can be daunted by the enormity of the concert hall.

My fear has always been performing at a church service where the organ pipes can be 20 to 40 feet away, which makes it seem very lonely and naked not to have the other musicians close. Silly, as a church is one of the friendliest and most forgiving places to perform.

> **Repetition is the cure for most of our problems as musicians.**

The key to curing all these situational fears is adaptation through repetition. As one begins to know the expectations of any situation, one can go into that situation with a better comfort level.

Self-loathing and other truly psychological/ chemical maladies are bigger problems when considering fear. The musician feels that they will never be good enough. An exceptionally good psychologist is in order and perhaps even medication is required. Search out the right therapist, because the 10% rule applies here as well. Ninety percent of the mental health community will not be of any help for a profound and effective outcome.

If we can learn to perform without self-medication (i.e., drugs, alcohol, pills, "vitamin I," Inderal, etc.) we are better off. Eventually, if these self-prescribed solutions need to be eliminated, we have a bigger void to cross and more self-created anxieties to confront.

From my point of view, performance anxiety is not the same as fear.

Fear is the dread of performing (or even rehearsing) in front of other people. Fear can come with many physical symptoms, including severe shaking, upset stomach (even vomiting on occasion), and countless other problems, both immediately before a performance or well in advance of a performance.

Performance anxiety is a result of the desire to perform as perfectly and beautifully as humanly possible. The body, to fine-tune perception, gives a shot of adrenaline to the performer, to create microscopic awareness. This state can create the feeling of "butterflies," or create a feeling of strength and concentration locking out all unnecessary distractions.

We must still try to control this performance anxiety through slow deep breathing and mental immersion in the task at hand.

There are a few lucky characters that are "cool as a cucumber" with "nerves of steel." These are people who have a natural sense of well-being and confidence and are extremely prepared with the material. They intrinsically feel that on any given day, no one could perform better than them.

There are those too, who have no fear because music does not have a special meaning, or they are not perfectionists. It may be a hobby, or they may be just doing it for their own amazement. They never expect to be advanced nor desire the personal growth music brings. They may play a section part in a community band and never desire a solo position. This is good! There is an important place for these fine people amongst those striving towards a professional career.

Many of us pursue music because music charms us. Some pursue music because they love to perform. The fear factor for those who love to perform is less than for those performers who love the approval of the audience.

To be a musician, we must learn to control our fear and anxiety or ignore it, if possible. In any case, we all must "play through it" occasionally. We must just "gut it out" and go out and do our job (perform).

Meditation? Prayer? Pep talks? Perhaps! Whatever works is good.

It seems that the whole subject is psychological in nature, doesn't it? The internal dialogue is brought to the forefront.

The best weight you'll ever lose
is the weight of other people's opinion of you.
—Susmita Nath

CHAPTER 7

Concepts

**Our concepts are the sum total
of our thoughts and experiences.**

We are mostly what we are taught, what we think, what we experience, and what new concepts (or abstract ideas) we are willing to accept.

Concepts are ever-changing.

Chance favors a prepared mind.
—Louis Pasteur

Our concepts are shaped in our early lives by our parents and significant people around us. Our own ideas are many times overridden by parents, often with the best of intentions or to have us adhere to their concept. As you age, you will find that you reassess your own ideas and concepts every few years. After all, they are your concepts, no matter where you get them, that control your life and opportunities.

An example *(this may be controversial)* is religion. Those youngsters with religious parents or parents who think religion may be important in the child's development will many times have a religion picked out for them based on the parent's concept of religion. Seldom is the child led to explore diverse religions to pick one or none for themselves.

While the child may change or abandon religion later in life, the concept of religion is difficult to change later in life.

I use this example not to criticize or pontificate, but to show the power of what we are taught in our formative years.

In most cases, the child will retain some form of relationship with the early religious training throughout life. That relationship may be strict adherence or may exhibit any number of variables of commitment. Someone who comes to a religious experience later in life will have a different relationship and concept of religion. The choice would more likely motivated by themselves rather than by a guardian.

If a young instrumentalist has their formative training from a classical teacher for a good period of time, the chances are that the student will become a classical musician, having learned from the classical perspective. Unless those teachers also have the concept of jazz, pop music, ethnic music, or whatever, the likelihood of the student veering from the classical path lessens.

The concept is also influenced by geography. In East India, for instance, what is heard on the radio, on television, and taught in East Indian music schools, will lessen the chances of a student becoming a European-styled classical musician.

Ultimately each person is responsible for their own concepts, their own growth of concepts, and what outcomes they produce from those concepts.

Concepts enter every subject in this writing. My concept in writing it and what I have decided to include and omit is my concept. Your concept of what I have said and what you will accept or reject from what I have written is the outcome of this discussion of concepts.

Concepts control our relationships with other people (social and business). Concepts control our relationship with ourselves. Concepts control what we do and how we do what we do.

How important are concepts?

Concepts influence our emotions, our ethics, and our being.

The symbols we use daily for communicating affect our concepts. Letters, numbers, visual symbols, aural teachings, and mental images all influence our concept.

When I was in fourth grade and trying to memorize the "Star Spangled Banner," my neighbor told me that she would rather I not practice that song while she was home. She said she felt she had to stand while I was practicing it. What a powerful illustration that is of music triggering a concept. She was serious!

Listening and witnessing life with mental stillness, a lack of internal dialogue, or thinking, is a valuable tool. To hear, view, or feel something without triggering a thought allows us to experience new concepts and experiences without the clutter of our old concepts.

Most musicians have had the experience of playing with "no mind." They have been "at one" with the music—not thinking, only reacting. It's a timeless feeling. A spiritual understanding, if you will. A feeling that keeps many of us pursuing a repeat of the experience.

Playing with "no mind" needs to be practiced. Long tones are a suitable time to practice "no mind," and sitting motionless is a suitable time to practice "no mind." Any time is a suitable time to practice "no mind"! "No Mind" simply means not talking to yourself while doing any activity.

For a musician, it is important to constantly grow our concepts. We must widen our field of experience and thought, so we can bring more understanding to our music. This growth of concepts includes growth in technical ability, emotional ability, listening ability, and in our communication.

How important are our concepts?

Our concepts are everything.

> *I am an old man and have known*
> *a great many troubles,*
> *but most of them never happened.*
> **—Mark Twain**

CHAPTER 8

Phrasing

Phrasing is the most important thing we need to understand to become a "finished" musician. A musician who is not just reading notes but taking the notes off the page and grouping them together to make the most sense, beauty, or understanding from them is a finished musician.

Have you noticed that almost every soloist, whether it's classical music, jazz, swing, county rock, or any other genre, is playing by memory? Why? It's the safest way to take the music off the page.

I am not saying that it's a necessity, but it's certainly a guaranteed way not to depend on the written note.

There are many musicians who can take the music off the page while still looking at or reading the notes. Studio musicians do that every day. Show musicians and celebrity accompaniment musicians do it all the time. Orchestral musicians do it, as do concert band musicians. Chamber musicians do it often too. It is possible.

So, what do I mean by "music off of the page"?

When we learn our first note, we see the note, give it a name, and learn the fingering. It may take a long time before we get to the point where we don't need to look at the notes, figure out the note name in our head, and then remember the fingering.

When you can look at a single note and your fingers embrace the note with no thoughts, you have *taken the note off the page*. Gaze at the note and play it without thinking. So, *not thinking* is what you need to do to play a note as the first step toward *taking the music off the page*.

But wait...there is more.

Then over the years, you get to the point where you can do that for every note on your instrument.

But wait...there is even more.

With three notes, you can play "Mary Had a Little Lamb." After you can play that simple tune without thinking or looking at the music, you have started to take it off the page.

But wait...there is even more yet!

Where are you going to breathe and what notes are you going to marry to each other?

Which of these phrasings is best?

"Mary, had a little lamb"?

Or

"Mary had, a little lamb"?

Or

"Mary had a, little lamb"?

Or

"Mary had a little, lamb"?

Or

"Mary had a little lamb"?

That decision turns simply taking the music off the page, into actually making music out of the notes. That is phrasing, the secret to being a finished musician.

Now all you must do is make those decisions on every phrase or grouping of notes you play.

A bar line is like a prison cell.
—András Schiff

But wait...there is more. Yikes!!

What about dynamics?

What about character?

What about endurance?

What about your internal dialogue?

What about touch? Yes, how do you touch your instrument?

What about playing with others?

What about rests?

What about listening?

What about your physical approach?

And that, my friends, is why we practice—to take "Mary Had a Little Lamb" off the page and own it with our body and non-thinking mind. The first step in a long journey. As are all the other steps. We are finally *singing*.

Learn to sing what you play.

Currently, I am playing in a new chamber group. I told one of the members it would be at least a year before we would be ready to perform or record. I don't think he believed me, but one day he said, "I see what you mean about taking a year." And we were only looking seriously at two pieces. As we get to know each other's playing better, we will gradually increase our repertoire.

One of my pet peeves is three or more *great* musicians playing chamber music that they may have practiced at home, but practicing as an ensemble has been minimal. The recording sounds great to the untrained ear, as the listener is as in love with the musicians as well as with the presentation. But to the trained ear, it is seldom cohesive music. And add a sound mixer who doesn't know the subtleties of chamber music, and you have a disaster that sells a lot of recordings.

CHAPTER 9

Intonation

For our purposes here, intonation is much more than simply playing "in tune." That is, just matching the vibrations of two or more notes.

Intonation *includes* volume, approach, nuance, tone color, flexibility, and yes, vibration.

Pitch and intonation for a wind and string musician is a malleable and moveable study.

Be willing to drive a "soft bargain" with intonation.

Pitch is *affected* by acoustics, temperature, humidity, the equipment that we use, and those around us.

In this modern-day of electrical tuners, it's important to tune your instrument to an A or Bb. And if you are only working on intonation with the tuner, it is something you can take time to learn—to nail the green light.

Please, please, *please* don't take your tuner to a rehearsal or to work and keep looking at it. Learn to hear the pitch and adjust to those around you when you can.

And don't tell your stand partner they are wrong because you are playing with the tuner, and they are not in tune with you. When you are playing with others, meet halfway on the pitch, always.

Did I say always? Yes, *always*. Two or more players trying to gravitate to the same pitch is the essence of intonation.

> *Your job as a musician is to make those*
> *players around you sound good.*
> **—Buddy Collette**

CHAPTER 10

Business

We are paid to be early—the music is for free!

A friend of mine likes to say, "Be plenty early, sit down, shut up." Stark, but to the point.

That's what the contractor, composer, and conductor want to see and hear.

Music is not a team sport, where if a player is not there, there is a substitute that must be called. The music keeps going with a hole in the harmony.

It's difficult to find a substitute for an open chair in the last moments before a recording session, or any rehearsal or performance, for that matter. In music, every chair is important. If a musician is not there to play their part, there is a hole in the performance.

It is also in extremely poor form to have to walk on stage during a performance. If you want to be hired again, respect the leader and contractor by being on the premises of a rehearsal or performance a half-hour before the event, and be ready to play 15 minutes before the downbeat.

Allow for traffic or a flat tire.

In performance, the business of music is everything—in addition to playing the notes.

Most things that are not music are business hurdles, some of which we must embrace.

My course on the business of music, a course that may help you understand what you need to do to be successful, is available at **www.iClassical-Academy.com**. So, I will be brief on this subject and trust that you will go to iClassical-Academy to watch my 9-episode presentation on the business of music.

Dan Jacobs's books, *The Natural Laws of Selling* and *The Natural Laws of Closing* are also must reads for not only every musician, but every person.

Business and selling are mostly interpersonal relationships that we encounter every day. So, it's good to study business and our relationships with people daily. Every musician is actually in business for themselves.

Make no mistake, most things you do every day involve selling or closing. And I will add to that, documenting an official deal requires a written contract. Also, don't forget to take notes. Keep a notepad next to your telephone. Notes become documentation, in case you ever end up in court on a dispute.

Remember, it's important to be there. Where? Where working people are spending time together both socially and in the work environment. Become their friend, not a get-me-a-job friend, but a real friend.

If you are in college, be where the college musicians spend time together. Your steady practice routines prepare you for work. *Recommendations get you work!* The more musicians you are real friends with, the better your chance of working. Even the musicians who you played with in elementary and secondary school will be in your life for a long time and they are the ones that might just take you to some great musical experiences.

DON'T FORGET,
THERE IS *YOUR* BUSINESS
AND *THE* BUSINESS

I have given you a couple of ideas about dealing with your own personal business in music.

What I want to talk about now is the business of music in general. This business is changing radically—with modern technologies and with corporations finding ways to purchase music for less almost daily. One thing is for sure, musicians and those who represent musicians, are not particularly good at standing up for themselves. Musicians are also not good at knowing their value (how much they should be paid).

Unfortunately, this will affect popular music, stage shows, ethnic music, jazz, recordings on both audio and video, television, motion pictures, and every genre of popular music you can think of. The governments in most countries are so mired in other dilemmas that the problems of musicians and music seem far down their list.

Because of the long history of classical music, and an audience that is much more sophisticated, I feel there will be less change in this genre of music. But as a warning to classical musicians, keep your eyes open to changes and deal with them early on if they do occur. We have already seen major orchestras in the United States declare bankruptcy, yet they find a way to go on.

Remember, that despite a government's desire to help you, you are far down on their list.

You and your employers must carry the banner for your success.

There is one dilemma in our business that's undeniable. There is always someone exceptionally talented who is willing to do your job for less money. That is where a union comes in—to try to hold the standards high. The best musicians tend to be in the union or higher echelon social groups. Though I must say that most union musicians seem to have no problem working without a contract. This, of course, lowers the general standard. As soon as employers figure out they can hire musicians for less than union scale, they do it.

Always work with a contract. It's not because you and the employer don't trust each other. Contracts in the music business seldom end up in court. The contract reminds everyone what the agreement was, set in words. Again, I suggest you watch my iClassical-Academy.com presentation on this matter.

If you will work for a little less every year,
you can stay in the entertainment field
the rest of your life.
—**Gary Mule Deer**

CHAPTER 11

On Genius

If we were destined to be a genius, a Mozart or a Bach, we would be there already, and would not have to worry about practicing. For most of us mortals, the steady path is best.

By the time he was 20, between his various gigs including jamming and practicing, by any conservative estimate, Charlie Parker had put no less than 15,000 hours into the saxophone.

That is another kind of genius—very hard work.

Many people consider Charlie "Yardbird" Parker a genius. Ross Russell in his biography, *Bird Lives*, describes his genius this way: "He was determined, dedicated, tireless, and ambitious." That, my friends, is the reality for most of us.

CHAPTER 12

Music Contracting

Music contracting is simply the job of hiring musicians. The caveat is that there are a lot of different types of music contractors. And there is an art to it. Also, legally, if there is litigation on any issue that is regarding the musicians the contractor hires, the contractor is considered to be a member of management and not a part of the orchestra. This is no matter if it's a playing contractor or a non-playing contractor.

There is the symphony music contractor, or in symphonic terms, orchestra manager, or personnel manager. The orchestra contractor should be a musician or if necessary, can be an administrator that assumes the job.

Symphonic orchestra managers must work within the contract the orchestra has with the union, or directly with the musicians. Musicians are mostly hired by audition and there may even be an approved substitute list. The real value of the orchestra manager is when the substitute list is exhausted or when a non-orchestral instrument is needed, then their contacts become important. As with most music contractors, they are the liaison between the union, orchestra management, and the musicians.

Let's discuss the motion picture or recording contractor. I am going to talk about the United States now, as my experience with European contractors was in the early 1970s, and I have no experience anywhere else in the world. There are the contractors that are known as "The Secretaries."

A bit of background:

Through the 1970s, there were contractors that at one point in their career were working musicians themselves (or may still be). Due to the volume of work, they all had secretaries who helped them with their paperwork. As these musician contractors retired or died, the secretaries would take over the positions since they knew the musicians that were being used and knew how to do the paperwork. In the meantime, they were in the booth interacting with the employers as well as the composers.

There are still working musicians that act as contractors. Good orchestras are provided by both musician contractors and secretary contractors. It must be said, when new musicians are introduced into the business, they have a better chance with the musician contractors or principal players than with the secretary contractors. The secretary contractors seldom, if ever, know the training required of the musicians or in the different styles of music the musician must possess.

The motion picture and record business were mostly done in Hollywood, California, and New York City for many years, but since about 1990, more and more work has gone elsewhere. The work has tended to migrate to England and Europe, Asia, South America, San Francisco, and other places where there are large numbers of qualified musicians.

In the United States, especially at the beginning of the recording business, thanks to Union President James Petrillo, most of the work was union and paid well, including benefits such as retirement and health insurance. Currently, as of the writing of this book, recording sessions are evenly divided between union and non-union jobs. Many of the non-union jobs are being taken by union musicians who do not take their membership seriously.

And now there is the new genre of computer-generated music where only one person is the whole orchestra, although they will occasionally hire a "real" solo musician or musicians to give life to the score and the frailty a live instrument brings to the sound.

Then there are contractors for live events, and there are the theater music contractors. Due to the varied instrumentation for Broadway musicals, these contractors might hire completely different orchestras based on the show and instrumentation required. They must know the local musicians well, as the musical style becomes very important. They must know musicians that play the standard instruments as well as the specialty instruments, like Pan Pipes, etc.

There are also contractors that work for music centers that require celebrity accompaniment in addition to Broadway shows and opera, and so on.

That's where I was employed, at the Cerritos Center for the Performing Arts, for thirty years before my retirement. At the time I retired in 2020, which was the beginning of the Covid epidemic, more and more "acts" were coming in self-contained. These same "acts" would previously come to the theater with key players, and the contractor would fill out the orchestra with local musicians. The economy is making it more difficult to hire local musicians.

When the union has a contract with the theater, they must adhere and hire a certain number of musicians for many shows, even if there is no music for them to play. These musicians are called *walkers*; they come in before every show, sign in, and then are free to go home or do whatever they want.

There are two important considerations to hiring a musician: Talent and character.

The worst thing a contractor can do is to create chaos amongst the musicians. For instance, you don't want two musicians who hate each other sitting next to each other. The smaller the section, the more important this becomes.

In a large string section, it's easy to put musicians that don't have an affinity for each other physically far apart. But in smaller sections, musicians are in close proximity. In a string section, it is the proper etiquette to consult the concert master on their preference. However, the final decision is that of the contractor.

Music contracting is the art of hiring to get the best sound.

For example, having four lead trumpet players in the same section is a roadmap for disaster. It's much better to have a first trumpet who can play high, if necessary, then a good 2nd trumpet backup; a solid 3rd and 4th trumpet for "in the staff" playing, and a 3rd or 4th player who can be an excellent improviser. It's important that each trumpet player understands how his or her part fits in the section. In the classical world, this is all taken care of primarily by the audition process.

Another example is the art of *not hiring* a string section of "concertmasters," as that would be disastrous too! All of the musicians in every section should get along and understand their place, not only in their own section, but in the ensemble as a whole.

There needs to be leaders and supporters in the correct proportion for every section.

The advantage of a larger section is that musicians who are not the best of friends can be seated apart from each other. It was always my method in contracting to hire the best musicians I knew for the job, and to balance the section with musicians who got along well and were great musicians in their own right. If they were my friend, all the better. But be careful, never hire only on the basis of friendship. It's interesting that once a contractor retires, he or she finds out who their real friends are.

CHAPTER 13

Listening

Sound goes two ways. In and out. Listening is something you hear from another source. It comes into your ear, and you process it. While you are playing, you are listening *(I hope)* and when someone else is playing, you listen. When someone talks—listen, and don't interrupt with your own opinion. You can learn much more by listening than by talking. However, of course, talking is a two-way exchange much of the time, so don't be afraid to be in the conversation. Just try not to control the conversation. If no one is talking, there are many sounds to hear. Life is seldom absolutely silent.

Be a good listener.
Give extra attention to a voice of importance.
—Jim Rohn

You send your sound out when you talk, sing, play an instrument, or scratch on a blackboard.

Remember that the sound is inside until you decide to let it come out. Also remember, if you keep your thoughts inside your head and no one hears them, you are not responsible for your thoughts. As soon as you say something, the world owns your words. So, think—or prepare—before you speak. The same goes for performances. Be prepared when you play, speak, or sing your first utterance as that is the first thing other people will remember. Your first note or utterance is always the most important.

And silence has a sound too.

> *A person with a talent for listening*
> *can hear things not yet spoken.*
> **—Gary Jennings**

Listen to music for enjoyment and listen to music to learn.

Active listening, also called dedicated listening, is where you are studying to grow as a musician.

In active listening, you may even be following a study score. Following a score is important, because you see the other parts, even if it's just a piano part. Very few musicians study that way because they are not taught that way. It's an advantage to listen with a score if you are studying written music. But active listening is just that. Don't be around other noise while you are doing it.

Again, remember there is a difference between thinking something and saying that same thing. Once you have said something, it becomes available to the whole world. Make your words kind, if you can.

Get out of your house and listen to live music. It's very different in spirit and educational value.

When you listen just for enjoyment or to create an atmosphere, you are most often creating sound as a background. When you're with other people, there may even be some comments about the music. Someone might give you a tip that helps you listen to the music. But then is not time to study music, rather it's time to bathe yourself, your space, and your friends and family in an atmosphere.

> *The music is not in the notes,*
> *but in the silence between.*
> **—Mozart**

> *What is best in music*
> *is not to be found in the notess.*
> **—Gustav Mahler**

CHAPTER 14

Ramblings

HOW TO STUDY OR PRACTICE

A desire to learn through study is essential to becoming an accomplished musician.

Practice, sometimes called study, or other more pleasant words are enlightening, rewarding, and uplifting.

Studying is also time-consuming and occasionally tedious.

> *Be eager to learn.*
> **—Jim Rohn**

Once a steady practice schedule is established and maintained for a while, it becomes a safe haven.

In making practice a regular routine, it's ideal for the practice session to be at the same time each day. Making it the first event of the day is one way to ensure that your practice session takes place on a regular basis.

Now when I say regular, some of the most motivated will immediately translate that concept into seven days per week. While practicing seven days a week is a noble undertaking, and even with the thought that some might be able to maintain that schedule on a long-term basis, I believe that a more moderate schedule is in order.

Perhaps five or six days a week of practice is ideal. The main idea is that regular practice becomes routine.

Oh, and take a week or two off occasionally. There is much to learn on days off, or on vacation. That's the time you relax and let all the work you have done come alive. You can clear your mind of the challenging work and feel the improvement you have made, while you have a great time and meet new people.

How long should one practice? My answer is that we should practice a minimum amount daily to achieve our goals. After we have reached our minimum time, we should continue practicing as long as the practice session keeps our interest, or how our schedule allows. The short answer is to play a minimum of one minute per session.

Get the instrument out of the case, put it together, and have some moments of silence. Practice your one minute, and if you want to do more, that's even better. If you try this day after day and aren't successful, this may not be the time for you to be studying music.

> **Play a minimum of one minute per practice session Do it on a regular basis.**

Look at it this way. Let's say hypothetically that it takes 20,000 hours to become a competent musician. One could practice 1,000 hours a year for 20 years, 2,000 hours a year for 10 years, or 4,000 hours a year for 5 years. Of course, there are all kinds of variations to this scenario, but the fact is, much of the decision or time commitment will come from the temperament of the student and the goal they are seeking. I have found that students that have been lackadaisical in their studies up the quality of practice about two years before they go to college. Fear it seems, is a great motivator.

I repeat. Consistency of practice is more important than the duration of practice. This cannot be stressed enough. Routine, Routine, Routine!

REMEMBER:
WE BECOME WHAT WE PRACTICE ON A DAILY BASIS.

Within the daily routine of practice, it's most advantageous that each practice session has a routine. This methodical approach facilitates the fastest and most consistent results.

Generally, it's good to start with a warm-up of some sort. This is not just for the muscles, but to center the mind.

Have a routine for your daily study time.

Next, do some technical work to methodically increase facility. Remember that studies are music too, so don't treat them like exercises. Play them musically. They don't have to be "in time" all the time.

Following the technical work comes time to work on the literature. Play the whole piece through first. Then work on technical or phrasing problems individually throughout the piece. Then end by playing the piece completely through again.

When playing the literature completely through, assume that someone is listening and that you are in performance. This approach prepares us to know what to expect of our performance before we must play in front of an audience.

Practicing and learning literature, whether it be jazz tunes, rock tunes, sonatas, concertos, symphonic literature, or literature of any type, is the crux of what studying is about.

> *The only alternative an artist has to*
> *not being himself is being nobody.*
> **—Roger Sessions**

Studying the literature in a methodical way gives us an opportunity for an overview of the piece, an opportunity to work on technical and aesthetic understanding, and then a review to assess our improvement.

The learning and even some memorizing of literature should begin as soon as a student is able to perform the basic tasks on the instrument. To a fourth grader, "Mary Had a Little Lamb" is their literature and should be treated as such. Including memorizing.

For woodwind doublers, the task of a practice routine for each session is a little more complex, and usually a little more time-consuming. This is especially true if doubling on three or four instruments.

What I will strongly suggest from my own experience, is that unless the flute was your first and primary instrument, practice the flute first, at least for the first few years of including the flute in your arsenal of tools. After the practice of other single- or double-reed instruments, go back to the flute for a few minutes at the end of the practice session to get a feel for playing on a swollen embouchure. The flute is the only instrument in the woodwind family that is not played by putting the instrument in the player's mouth. That is a huge difference.

Ideally, a woodwind doubler should practice instruments from each family of instruments at each practice session. Few doublers have the time and energy to play 3 or 4 families of instruments each practice session. It's important, however, to play more than one family of instruments as often as possible in a practice session.

Another suggestion for doublers (as well as single-instrument musicians) is to leave the instruments out on an instrument stand unless there is some danger to the instruments in doing so. Otherwise, take them out of the case as soon as you get home or to your studio. The instrument that's out of the case is begging to be played. If you leave your case open, you minimize the chance of taking an empty case to a rehearsal or worse yet, to a performance.

The doubler is best served by considering the practice routine suggested herein and pursuing that routine perhaps except for an extended warm-up procedure. After the complete routine on each instrument, spend some time going back and forth with the instruments that are out with very little time between instrument changes.

I will say again that doublers should study with single-instrument players, in addition to any doubler they are studying with.

A dedicated oboe player will give you much more insight into making an oboe or English horn reed than a doubler. To get a great flute sound it's almost mandatory to study with a straight flute player.

It's important to live our life and progress musically from our own experiences. We must listen to what others say, tell us, or advise us; however, it's best not to take this advice as gospel. Consider the information, evaluate the information, and digest the information, and only upon finding one's own truth from the information, believe that information. Also, always consider the source of the information!

Learning is the new form of labor.
—Shoshana Zuboff

SAVE YOUR MONEY

I keep saying that. So, I must think it's important. Learn about money.

Thank those who came before you and nurture those who come after you. Even after you leave a teacher and move on for some reason or another, call that teacher and thank them again from time to time. They deserve it, and you will feel good that you did it.

How did your parents shape your life? This is an especially important thing to consider if you are to be your own person in adulthood. Don't shy away from examining your past. You are very lucky if you were born to good parents who didn't abuse you and, in fact, encouraged you. Though you will be tempted to believe everything your parents told you when you were young, examine those ideas as you get older, and take from their advice only the things you know to be true, from your examination of a subject, and not theirs. I'm sure your parents advised you based on their knowledge and experience, including the knowledge their parents passed to them. Make sure that the information you take from them is fact and not just an opinion.

Your opinion is not necessarily my truth.
—Sandy Pringle

I see little difference between practicing and performing. Performing just seems to me as simply practicing in front of other people. Sometimes performance is a bigger lesson than practicing alone.

The difficulty of music: Be kind to others who are not as good as you and learn from those who are better than you.

Ethics – I hope you have them.

> *Be kind.*
> *Everyone you meet is fighting*
> *a hard battle you know nothing about.*
> **—Plato**

Competition is the best way to get better quickly, and the worst way to love music. If you *must* compete, have Humanity and Compassion.

CHAPTER 15

Options to Performing

What are some other music-related things the performer can do?

- Composing
- Arranging
- Audio recording
- Live audio
- Video recording
- Teaching
- Music theory
- Instrument repair
- Working in a music store
- Owning a music store
- Tonemiester
- Concert production
- Agent or agency
- Record company
- Music supervisors
- Computer expert
- Reviewer, etc.

I asked my elementary school music teacher what was the most important thing in music. He said, "be good at more than one thing." So, the suggestions above are ideas about how you can find other music-related things to do.

This is just the start of many avenues to pursue if you find out you can't make a living on your instrument. Use your creativity to find a place for yourself in our business. Play part time as it keeps your chops up and is so much fun.

You will get to hear a whole bunch of music. I have purposely left out being a DJ, as they steal our music and never think twice about it.

No matter what you think it's going to be,
it's going to be something different.
—Jack Reidling

PART TWO

Ezines
Electronic Magazines

My Ezine, or Electronic Magazine, is something I started a few years ago with the help of a great musician, Jon Kip, who knows the computer well. I attempt to broadcast to my Internet mailing list every two months or so, trying not to make it a music lesson, per se, but to have my one-sided conversation relate to the problems of being a woodwind musician (or a musician of any genre or instrument). I like to talk about issues in the business of music and about the interactions of people. I hope the readers understand, at least the professional ones, that they are in business and it needs to be treated like a business. So here are all the Ezines up to the date of the publishing of this book. You can sign on at **www.mikevaccaro.com** to subscribe.

If you have read the previous part of this book, you will recognize much of what was said and, in some cases, repeated here. There are issues that I raise here that were not included in the previous section. So, use this section as a kind of review and get some new related information. Also, there are subjects not talked about previously in this book, with some brand new insights. So, it's worth taking the time to read through them all. Please do not assume that because you recognize some of the language in the Ezines that the message is exactly the same.

I urge you to not read through these quickly. Read one think about it and see if you agree with these ideas.

Reeds and Mouthpieces

Welcome to the first offering of my musings. Today, I would like to talk for a moment about reeds and their importance, both in performing and in selecting a new mouthpiece.

I was recently informed by a representative of one of the major reed manufacturers that reeds are coming in about a half size stiffer than in the past, and he sees this likely to happen for a few years to come. I have personally found this trend to be true regarding the various brands of reeds that I've recently played, and if you are having difficulties finding a good reed, my advice is to try a softer strength than you normally play. Of course, you also need to determine if your mouthpiece is part of the problem.

As with wine, cane is different from year to year—and from region to region. The quality of the reeds being manufactured by any company is subject to the crops of cane that are available for that particular year. And it can be expected that cane will be different from company to company, depending on where they buy their cane.

It's important to remember that different companies get their cane from various parts of the world, mostly the Var region of France, but also from many other sources. For instance, South America is a major new player in the cane game. There are also many new reed companies. The smaller companies don't have the need to sell as many reeds, so they tend to be more particular about which part of the cane shaft they use and how the cane is aged and cut. Also, some of the larger, better known companies are marketing higher-end products that claim to be more refined and exceptional compared to their standard lines.

Because of the many changes in cane around the world, **it's important not to get married to a particular brand of reed** just because you have used it all your life or your teacher tells you that's the cane to buy. **Experiment!!!!!**

I was using Eastman Reeds (as of this Ezine writing, 2023, Eastman seems to be out of the reed business, so I am using other brands), and I am finding a high percentage of excellent reeds per box, a great response, a complex tone, and comfort on my mouthpiece with the various reeds I am using. I repeat that is *now*. Next year or the year after, I may find a cane that works better, so it helps to keep an open mind and to compare your current reed to other available brands, especially if you aren't getting good reeds on a regular basis.

I played clarinets, saxes, flutes, and oboes during my working career. I used a different brand of reed on most instruments *(no, not the flute)* and within the family of instruments.

I will go into reed adjustment and its importance on another occasion, however, if you are unsure of how to modify your reeds for the ultimate playing experience, I strongly suggest that you purchase Tom Ridenour's reed system, which can be found online at **www.ridenourclarinetproducts.com/ATG1.html** or from the retailer of your choice. I suggest you buy the complete package with video and workbook, plus, of course, the reed tool. This system can make even the beginner adept at reed modification. Since I also play the oboe, I tend to use a knife and sandpaper instead.

FINDING A REED FOR A NEW MOUTHPIECE

The first thing to do is to take some new reeds and make them so that they respond on your old mouthpiece—but don't fine-tune them yet. With these reeds, some of which may be too hard or too soft, you're in the position where you know you have somewhat responsive reeds to try on potential new mouthpieces. You're at least in the ballpark.

After you have selected a mouthpiece with these new reeds, play and adjust them for optimum sound and response. It has been my experience that musicians do not usually make radical changes in their mouthpieces. Big changes usually come over a period of time. That said, even a change of a few thousandths of an inch in the tip opening or in the length of the facing, can make the mouthpiece play much differently. Even though a new mouthpiece may feel good at first, you still have to learn how to play it, as it's bound to be different from your old mouthpiece. Only then will you know the true potential of your new equipment.

Life is A Gift...

As part of these articles, I like to give you some thoughts that might improve your playing or the playing of your students. This Ezine is about a great book, *Life Is a Gift: The Zen Of Bennett*.

We all are helped by inspirational books. You may have read *The Art Spirit* by Robert Henry, *Effortless Mastery* by Kenny Werner, or many of the other books that are not musical notes to practice, but rather words to ponder. These books help our mental game by improving our playing through learning to *think about music and life differently*.

I have always kept a journal where I collect positive thoughts to inspire myself. I find that learning to see life through the eyes of people with different experiences is very helpful.

I am happy to say that pop icon, Tony Bennett, has written a great book, *Life Is a Gift*, about his career and the lessons he learned along the way. I strongly suggest you purchase this inspirational read.

Here are a few quotes from his book:

"It takes ten years to learn how to walk out on stage."

"Choose a career that you gravitate to naturally."

"Do something to improve yourself every day."

"Instead of focusing on being number one, attempt to be one of the best."

"When you choose your friends, realize that you are choosing your teachers."

"The definition of a true friend is someone that is happy for your success."

"It's very important to learn what to leave out, thereby emphasizing what remains."

"It takes years of practice to make our best work seem effortless."

These quotes are from just the first chapter, so you can imagine the number of lessons to be learned by digesting the whole book.

When you choose your friends,
realize that you are choosing your teachers.
— Tony Bennett

#3

Silence

As part of these articles, I would like to give you some thoughts that might improve your playing or the playing of your students.

This time, we will talk about **SILENCE** *(quietly)*.

It has been said that, "music is a picture painted on a canvas of silence."

That's not always true these days but is desirable for those going to a concert hall, or in a chamber music setting. To some extent, this holds true for jazz concerts also.

As a musician, silence is important too. I once asked a trumpet player on a recording session why he never warmed up. He said, "I do it at home so as not to bother anyone else, and if I need to play a few notes just to make sure everything is working I use a mute." You can imagine, and I am sure you have experienced, 50 to 80 musicians "warming up" at full volume so you can't even hear yourself.

The professional motto has pretty much always been "be plenty early, sit down, and shut up." While sounding harsh, the general idea in any money-making situation is that there are other people around who need to be considered—the sound person, the stage crew, other musicians, a featured act, or any other position you can think of. Each has a job to do and constant blowing by musicians just before a job is insensitive and unnecessary. It's best to keep the ego at home and save your best playing for the performance and not the warm-up.

The same goes for practicing. To take the instrument out of the case and start playing your fastest and best licks helps no one, especially you. It's best to start practicing with a minute or two of silence after the instrument is put together, just to get all the thoughts of the day out of your head. Then you really have a chance of listening to the first note you play. The first note you play is always the most important note you play. Listen.

As you warm up or start to practice, try starting from that silence (*mental as well as physical*). Good times for using this silence are when practicing has not been going so well, if you need to think about how you want to play a phrase, or even if you are a little too tired from practicing and need a rest.

The bottom line is that we just don't leave enough time for silence in music and in our lives. So, what happens? We storm through life, never really looking closely at anything because we are trained to stay active. Only the act of little or no action **Listen.** gives us a chance to really observe. In other words, when we turn off our internal dialog and let our unconscious mind do its work unimpeded, we have a better chance of success.

It's very difficult to talk and listen at the same time. If we can avoid doing this, we learn more about the other person as well as about ourselves.

Take a moment to think about how silence can help you in your life.

#4

You and Your Instrument

Your instrument is an important part of your success in music. How well do you take care of your instrument and is your instrument of artistic quality?

I was reminded of this the other day after Paul Rabinov spent three hours on my instrument. When he handed it back to me, he said something like, "You must have been working hard to get the low notes."

Well, yes, I was, and when I then played the instrument and realized how easy it was to play, it reminded me yet again, that our instruments are so important to our success. After all, when it sounds easy, it usually is easy.

So many times, if you are like me, we blame ourselves first. Why can't I get that note? How come that phrase is so difficult? It's my reed. It's my headjoint. It's my mouthpiece. What do I need to do to make this music sound better? Well, sometimes the problem is us and sometimes the problem is our instrument.

If playing isn't fun anymore, or you seem to be losing your touch, your repairperson should be your first stop. In addition, you should just plan on a once-a-year total cleaning, oiling, and adjustment of your instrument.

Additionally, the time when the instrument is in peril and in need for adjustment is any time there is a radical weather change. Pads dry out or get wet, wood instruments swell and contract, and corks can start to crack, making it prime time for possible adjustments.

Find the best repairperson you can. If you don't know who to go to, ask your teacher. You want a woodwind specialist, not just a store where the repairperson repairs everything that comes in, from tubas to piccolos. It's possible that the music store repairperson can be good at everything; however, an expert on one instrument, your instrument, is the best person to look for.

Don't be afraid to drive a little farther or pay a little more for expertise. You will be happy, and your instrument will be happy, and all those musicians you play with will be happy too.

There are many types of new pads and resonators available for all woodwind instruments, especially flutes. Be sure to ask your repairperson if they are experienced with any new type of pad system. If not, call the instrument or pad company and find an authorized technician.

Make friends with your repairperson. Watch them work; you can learn a lot and get into some pretty engaging conversations too. You may even develop an interest in repair work yourself. It's always a good craft to know, even if it's just to get your instrument going in an emergency. In addition, with the music business in such a transitional period these days, with recorded music taking over where live music traditionally was used, having extra marketable skills can be useful.

Synthesizers are replacing musicians, not only in films, documentaries, and television, but in live music performances like Broadway pits, churches, and any venue you can think of. The improvement in the sounds available to synth composers is so impressive that I can't always tell if the music I'm hearing is created by a synthesizer or a group of single musicians.

The more musical skills you have, in addition to the ability to perform on an instrument, the better chance you have of staying close to music for a lifetime. Repair work is certainly one of those areas that need experts all over the country. A musical sideline never hurts your understanding of music.

So . . . keep your instruments in shape—to play better and have more fun.

Nerves, Fear, and Butterflies

Some people have no fear. They walk through life, taking it as it comes.

This talk is about the rest of us.

No one has a case of "the nerves" all the time. I never know when the butterflies are going to present themselves, but as I have aged, those times are fewer and farther apart. I guess that's what comes with age. An acceptance of our frailties, and, having stared down nerves, fear, and butterflies enough, it just seems not worth it. And finally, I really prepare for whatever musical journey is ahead.

That is why it's important not to shrink from "the nerves" and to stand up and play music every chance you get. The very best time to learn something is *before* you play in front of an audience. If necessary, you can learn "on the job" with enough repetition. In fact, even when you practice at home, it's good to imagine an audience listening to you practice.

Accept the trauma of truth.
—Jim Rohn

In a nutshell, nerves, or nervousness before a performance, whether it be solo or ensemble, is generally our self-worry about the outcome of our performance. It can also be caused by performing in a strange or new environment, an environment where we don't control our own circumstances as we are used to.

Perhaps we have not yet mastered our music to the point where we *can't* make a mistake, which is certainly a reason to be a bit nervous when walking on stage.

There are butterflies, which in general, is just our body going into high gear so we can microscopically attend to our playing with as much attention as we can muster. That's different from fear, which has debilitated many a great musician.

So a brief re-cap: It seems to me that in general, "real fear" comes from not being prepared, or not having confidence about our perform-ance situation, and butterflies are the body just gearing up to amplify our performance in our own mind, so we can listen more intensely and perform better.

Fear is the worry about the outcome of your performance *(will it be good enough for your standards or the audience's standards?)* or worry about how you will be perceived after the performance.

I am talking here about musicians who are generally psychologi-cally happy. Those that carry self-loathing around as a way of life should get professional help, as this article will be of little help to those with injured egos or those with unreasonable expectations.

Part of fear is knowing how well prepared you are for a performance and a real understanding of your progression in the art of music. If you have not practiced a piece until it meets your standards, your fear of failing is real and could likely happen. If you are a jazz/pop musician and have not really taken care to learn the chords to the piece you are going to improvise on, fear of failing is real again, and is a possibility.

As woodwind players, we are generally soloists, as opposed to being in a large string section or in a clarinet section in a concert band. So, understanding the importance of being a soloist is paramount. After a lot of practice to where you know you can play the solo every time *(in the ensemble or in front of it)*, it comes down to believing in yourself that you have something unique to contribute to the music.

Preparation is the number one prerequisite for minimizing or elim-inating nerves of the fear type. The first bottom line then is to know you are prepared to perform, either as part of the ensemble or as a featured soloist. You should prepare until you know that you can play your solo several times perfectly, or near perfectly *(which means not making the same mistake in the same place every time, which means you are at least consistent, but really not prepared*). If you *are* prepared, the butterflies will give you the concentration to play up to your best level or even better.

The next step for any featured soloist is to perform your music, as many times as you can, for as many people as you can, before the big performance. Then you will know how it feels to play in front of other people. That is acclimating to the performance experience.

At the same time, you must remember that nothing is really perfect. Your humanity is part of the performance and with preparation that humanity shows in a positive way.

Breath and airflow become a problem when nerves enter the picture. Slow breaths (full, but not forced or too deep) before walking out on stage, while concentrating on how beautifully you will play the first phrase, are helpful. Inhale slowly and exhale in the manner your body wants to naturally expel the breath. This is also a good technique when your practice isn't going well, to make sure you are not shallow breathing. For both practicing and performing, concentrating on the breath helps turn the internal dialogue off and cleanses you of negative thoughts.

Many times, as woodwind players, we forget how important breath is. The control of the breath is the soul of the sound and the heart of phrasing.

Tony Bennett says it takes 10 years to learn how to walk on stage. Most of us don't have the luxury of having those 10 years of doing 3 or more solo performances a week. So, we rely on preparation and a bit of fortitude. A smile...and acceptance of the audience doesn't hurt either.

The environment can cause nerves too. I remember having played with a chamber music group for several years and had no problem walking on the stage and performing solo and ensemble pieces. One night, the audience was within three feet of me, and could see me breathe, watch my fingers closely, and, in general, view me microscopically. That made me more nervous than performing for a thousand people. However, if that was the environment I always worked in, I would have already adjusted to it, and I would be able to better cope with the situation.

Some people would rather record music and some people prefer to make music in front of people. It's all about what you're used to.

Glen Gould, possibly one of the greatest soloists to live, quit performing live at the age of thirty. He called the piano soloist touring process "the last blood sport." He had another 20 years of great music-making in the recording environment, as a producer, director, and piano soloist before he passed.

It helps to be outgoing and to have the feeling that people are on your side, as this adds to the chance that all will go well in your performance.

For me, it seems that the true joy of performing is presenting music to a group of people. When we are presenting music, we are doing it for the audience or for our fellow musicians, and that helps take the microscope off ourselves. We are simply passing our gift of music on to someone else.

Remember to concentrate on what you are doing and not on the outcome. That will help stop any negative internal dialogue. Stay in the moment. We must grow as people beyond our anxieties. We must believe we have something to contribute.

Remember, there is always someone who plays better than you or is different than you. You are always better than someone else and have your own style. Music is not a competition.

If you practice on a regular basis, it's important to "be happy with where you are at, while you are trying to get where you want to be."

P.S. After writing this article, I saw a piece by Madison Sonnier that explains self-esteem, which is much about what this whole thing is about. Don't miss going to her website and reviewing this important message:

https://tinybuddha.com/blog/realizing-your-self-worth-and-believing-in-your-path/

I also suggest you sign on to Noa Kageyama's blog on performance and fear.

Reeds and Mouthpieces 2

The first thing you must realize when buying a saxophone or clarinet mouthpiece is how the reed affects your mouthpiece decision. If you use a reed that you like, and that is "married" to your mouthpiece, the only mouthpiece you'll favor will be a mouthpiece that is much like your own. I would assume you're looking for a new mouthpiece because you're trying to improve something in the *response, sound quality,* or *pitch* of your current setup.

It's best to have several good *new* reeds of different strengths to try a new clarinet or saxophone mouthpiece. A new reed will help determine the accuracy of the facing. Reeds of varying strengths will also make different facings play harder or easier, thus giving you an idea of what the mouthpiece requires.

It's ok if you must completely change your reed strength to accommodate a new mouthpiece. Remember, you are looking for something new and more appropriate for what *you* do!

Play for short periods. Play more melodic passages throughout the range of the instrument and check sound, intervals, and the ability of the mouthpiece to respond quickly between registers. Play slowly and listen carefully. Playing only quick, familiar patterns when testing a sax or clarinet mouthpiece can cover up any inherent shortcomings it may have.

First impressions are important. Remember, the mouthpiece is supposed to make the style and sound of the music you intend to play easier to produce.

You will *always* produce the sound that you hear in your head. The mouthpiece should make that easier.

Clarinet and saxophone mouthpieces are complex.

To take any measurement, whether it's the facing length, facing opening, or the internal features, and make that a criterion for your purchasing decision is an intellectual mistake.

It's how the mouthpiece *plays* and *makes your job easier* that counts, and not the measurements.

Remember, you are looking for something because most likely your mouthpiece does not make performing as easy as you want it to be.

Some performances require soft-playing clarinet or saxophone mouthpieces, and some performances require a mouthpiece that will project enough to reach the back of the hall. Know what you're looking for, and the purpose for which you are going to use the mouthpiece. Your performance area can have a lot of reverberation or be very dead, which enters into your decision.

Does your clarinet or saxophone reed work the way you want? Is it easy to find a clarinet or saxophone reed and keep them playing well? Those are the basic questions.

Let's start with this, is it easy to find a reed?

First, for a reed to work the table on your saxophone or clarinet mouthpiece must be perfectly flat and the curve of the facing must be one that complements your style of playing. If the mouthpiece is not correct, you have little chance of finding a reed on a regular basis.

Secondly, you must be playing a reed that is the correct size for your clarinet or saxophone mouthpiece setup. Of course, this can vary. I have heard it said we should play the softest reed we can, to get the job done...*and only YOU can decide if that works for you.*

I have found that many amateur and also professional musicians use a reed that is too hard and they end up suffering because of it.

Conversely, I find that most beginners start with a reed that's too soft, and stay on it much too long during their learning progress. Needless to say, the student must have an appropriate clarinet or sax mouthpiece that is easy to play, which is likely not the one that comes with the rental instrument or the first purchased instrument. A sax or clarinet mouthpiece is the least expensive component that I know of to promote fast learning.

If your sax or clarinet reeds are not working on a regular basis, or if you must go through a whole box of reeds or more to get *one* working reed, you're most likely using the wrong brand of saxophone or clarinet reeds!!!

With all the choices out there, start trying different brands of reeds. Don't be afraid to experiment! Don't use a certain brand of reed just because your teacher or your favorite musical artist does, or because that's what you have always used. A clarinet or saxophone reed source (brand) that has been good for a couple of years may not be good forever, so when your reeds start being a problem, it's time to search again.

Then there is the cane to consider. There are lots of differences in cane. The questions to consider: Where is the cane grown? What company or supplier is getting the best cane, aging it properly, and putting a good cut on it? If you have a good piece of cane for a sax or clarinet reed, you almost can't ruin it. If you have a terrible piece of cane for a reed, there is nothing you can do to fix it. Most sax and clarinet reeds fall in the middle of *great* or *horrible,* so you will have to adjust most reeds to work for you and your unique needs.

The reed companies come closer than you may think. There is no way they can know your particular needs though. The next item then, is your knowledge of the reed, how it works, and how to adjust it.

It was said of Benny Goodman, that before each concert, he would sit down with 10 or 15 boxes of clarinet reeds and play them all until he got one he liked.

For those of you who like to play a new sax or clarinet reed all the time, it's in your best interest to rub the vamp towards the tip, closing the cells of the reed to minimize the wet-dry cycle. If you don't do that, most certainly the next time you take it out of the reed case, it will be completely different.

There are several books on the market that you can find on the subject of reed adjustment, so I won't go into a reed symposium here. You can also get information on saxophone or clarinet reed adjustments from your teacher.

I do suggest the reed adjustment tool made by Tom Ridenour that is available at his website **www.ridenourclarinetproducts.com**, or from many retail outlets throughout the country. You can order just the tool; however, I suggest you get the instruction book and DVD that goes along with it. There is much insight to be found in Tom's method. Sometimes I use Tom's method and sometimes I just go after the adjustment with a great knife I bought from Bill Stevens and some wet and dry sandpaper. Being an oboe player for 50 years has given me an insight to cane adjustment that many single-reed players don't have.

As you get several years of experience working on your saxophone or clarinet reeds, you will find a consistency in your reeds that you may never have thought possible.

Remember, you can remove cane from a saxophone or clarinet reed, but you can't put it back on, so work slowly and keep trying the reed.

If you aren't an expert at adjusting a reed, you will forever find your reed a mystery.

Regarding synthetic saxophone or clarinet reeds, I must say I don't usually perform with them; however, I do keep a couple of them in my reed cases, just in case the weather is so difficult that the cane reeds are acting up. Another good use for these reeds is for outdoor concerts or when you need to play unreasonably loud. Although I don't use synthetic saxophone or clarinet reeds, I know several very successful professional musicians that use them almost exclusively and I must say I can't hear the difference in sound when they are using them.

Reeds are alive and they change every day based on humidity, temperature, and the fact that they are bamboo. It's in our best interest to learn how to minimize that change.

> **Remember - Most good reeds are *made* and
> not *found*, so, become an expert at adjusting reeds,
> and your life and music will become better.**

Why Aftermarket Products?

As the science of instrument building and the knowledge of acoustics have progressed, the needs and desires of instrumentalists to push the envelope on their performance skills have advanced as well. Adding to that, with the increased overall skill level of today's players with increased competition, players are looking for ways to gain an advantage.

One way is to improve their equipment. To meet this need, small businesses have sprung up with the goal of providing musicians with the equipment to help them achieve greater skills. While these products don't replace practicing, they do make your practicing easier and aid in faster learning and the enjoyment of music.

Some of these aftermarket products include:

- Clarinet and saxophone mouthpieces & ligatures
- Clarinet barrels and bells
- Saxophone necks
- Flute headjoints
- Neck straps for clarinet
- Rubber covers for the thumb rests
- Reed adjustment tools
- Ligatures

CLARINET MOUTHPIECES

You purchased a new or used instrument. If you purchased it with some knowledge of what you were looking for, it's likely you bought one much better than what you'd been using. So, if it *is* better, why consider aftermarket products like a barrel, bell, mouthpiece or even a ligature?

The simple answer is *because that clarinet can become even better.*

The fact is, if you try 20 or more clarinets, *one* will be much better than the others. And if you try 20 barrels, bells, mouthpieces, and ligatures, one of each will be better than the others. Guaranteed!

There are many sources for aftermarket clarinet products. Some of these products will work for you and some of them won't. If your goal is to sound as good as you possibly can and to play with greater ease, it's in your best interest to at least try them.

I can dare to say that almost any mouthpiece that comes with a new instrument will not do the job for you. Why is that? Simply put, the manufacturer does not know who you are, how you play, or where and in what situations you play. They are *instrument makers* and not *mouthpiece makers.*

Although it might be in their best interest to have a mouthpiece maker finishing a mouthpiece for at least their top-of-the-line clarinets, it's an expense they are just not willing to take on, as it's a very competitive market, and their job is to sell clarinets. The manufacturer also assumes you will have your own mouthpiece or will be looking for an alternate one.

Thus, the mouthpiece is most likely the first aftermarket product that you will be looking for.

SAXOPHONE NECKS

Saxophone necks act much like a clarinet barrel. It has only been in recent years that we've seen a variety of manufacturers and private makers producing fine aftermarket saxophone necks. For the same reasons as above regarding barrels and bells, if you are a saxophone player, you'll want to at least experiment with them.

FLUTE HEADJOINTS

The same can be said of flute headjoints. Though expensive, every professional flutist I know is in constant search for the perfect headjoint. Of course, those are the ones who have not found one yet.

THE UNENDING SEARCH?

Just think how lucky we would all be if the first instruments that touched our hands were perfect in every way. Having the right equipment to start with would save thousands of hours of hard work and suffering. Oh, well! If you are not that lucky, the search is on.

Woodwind Mouthpieces
Parts, Function, Concept

THE MOUTHPIECE

This text is a supplement to a video I did for Eastman Winds and includes some additional information that was left out of the video for various reasons. That video is available on YouTube by typing in my name, Mike Vaccaro.

I would like to talk about the mouthpiece, how it functions, and how to select the best one for you.

It's important to realize that the mouthpiece, reed, and ligature are a marriage that together determines the sound, approach, and response of your instrument.

Instrument makers are in the business of making woodwind instruments, and generally, not mouthpieces. I can say with certainty that the mouthpiece that comes with your instrument will either not play or will be inappropriate for your use. Why is this? Simply put, it's because the instrument maker does not know you, your playing style, your level of experience, nor the situations in which you perform.

The job of fitting a mouthpiece to any person is based on the trade-off between flexibility and stability in the mouthpiece, and the playing needs of that particular person.

The technology of mouthpieces has progressed at lightning speed over the past few years, and a specialist/mouthpiece maker who can match a mouthpiece to your needs and playing style can make your practicing easier and you won't end up with a shoebox full of useless mouthpieces over the years. Think of the money and aggravation you'll save!

You're Welcome!

It's much better to go in person to a mouthpiece craftsman than to go through the mail order process because the craftsman can watch and see how you play and help you assess your needs. Or, in the case of the beginner, can hand that person a mouthpiece that facilitates their fastest advancement.

In short, the craftsman can assess your manner of playing. Some musicians play very tight, some very loose. Some put a lot of mouthpiece in their mouth and some take very little. Some musicians blow a lot of air through the instrument, and some hardly any. Some musicians play with a tight body position and some play loosely. There are as many variables as there are players.

The mouthpiece maker also provides ears that are in *front* of the instrument and not *behind* it so they can give you input on the sound that they hear and what the audience hears. Many mouthpiece makers can play the mouthpiece for you on your instrument so you can hear it from a different perspective.

The correct mouthpiece will save you many hours of practice and money spent on reeds.

If you go to the music store and try 10 mouthpieces that are supposed to be exactly the same, one will play better than the others. Try that and find out. Or an aftermarket mouthpiece craftsman can introduce you to a custom mouthpiece that may be much better than the one you have selected.

It's like buying a custom-made shirt and suit or a custom pair of shoes. They just fit better.

These days mouthpieces are made from all types of materials: plastic, ebonite, hard or rod rubber, glass or crystal, wood, and metal of all types, to list just a few.

Some people don't think material matters in a mouthpiece, but I say if a mouthpiece was made out of cement, they might change their mind. Using extremes is sometimes a way to prove a point.

It has been my experience that most advanced classical clarinet and saxophone players have a general idea of the concept of what they want to sound like. Remember, I said *general* idea. Some are looking for a firmer approach and some are looking for a looser one.

With jazz and rock musicians, there is much more variance and acceptance of different sound concepts. There are even mouthpiece makers that cater to these specialty sound concepts.

WHAT IS THE PURPOSE OF A MOUTHPIECE?

For the beginner, the purpose of a mouthpiece is simply to easily get a sound, and the mouthpiece that came with the instrument, may or may not do that. Most likely *not*. A custom mouthpiece will do it better.

For the intermediate musician, the function of the mouthpiece is to be able to start to develop a style of playing based on interests, concepts, and reed preferences.

For the advanced musician, the goal is the refinement of sound and finding a mouthpiece that will facilitate the style of music they will be playing. The idea is to be able to adjust the nuances of the mouthpiece with a mouthpiece maker to develop different characteristics of sound (brightness, darkness, overtone series, etc.), air potentials (i.e. how easy the mouthpiece plays, air angle, and where the kickback starts), and even intonation.

> **What is true is that if a professional musician can't play on a student mouthpiece, what chance does a student have to excel on a student mouthpiece?**

Wouldn't it be great if the student could be handed their first mouthpiece and have it last a lifetime, making their journey easier, and saving them practice time, money, and frustration? That is possible now.

Checking in with a mouthpiece craftsman every few years can help you decide if your mouthpiece is still what you need, or if it could use a modification, or if a new mouthpiece is even what you need. Or even better yet, saying that no change is needed.

MOUTHPIECE NOMENCLATURE

Outside Mouthpiece Nomenclature:

Tenon—The bottom of the clarinet mouthpiece where the cork fits into the clarinet.

Shoulder—Where the tenon meets the mouthpiece body on a clarinet mouthpiece.

Body—The outside shape of the mouthpiece, including the density of the material from which it is made.

Beak—The part you put in your mouth. This is the top of the mouthpiece and can be shaped many ways. There are many designs that change the angle from the body of the mouthpiece to the tip of the mouthpiece. In short, the beak has an effect on comfort and tone. Mouthpiece patches change the angle of the outside curve and the effect of the response of the beak.

Bite—The bite is the part of the beak closest to the tip. It can be thick, medium, or thin. For the mouthpiece maker, the thin bite leaves little room for alterations, as the beak must have enough strength to support the embouchure. Once the bite has been compromised, it's very difficult for the mouthpiece maker to continue working on the mouthpiece.

Shank—The part of the sax mouthpiece that fits over the cork and correlates to the tenon on the clarinet.

Facing Nomenclature:

Table—Where the reed is placed to be secured by the ligature. It's very important that the table be flat (some mouthpiece makers make a concave area in the middle of the table, and claim that it creates suction with the reed. I prefer flat.) Flat tables are best for finding reeds. This eliminates an important variable. Mouthpieces that are bought in stores, or come with your instrument, are rarely flat, as they are made by machines and almost never hand finished. There are some mouthpieces that will work without flattening the table, but consider yourself lucky if you get one that works.

Window—The whole open part of the mouthpiece from the tip to the table.

Side Rails—The left and right rails that go towards the tip to the right and left of the window.

Tip Rail—The area at the tip of the mouthpiece at the top of the window.

Tip Corners—Where the side rails meet the tip rail.

Throat—Where the chamber meets the bore.

Facing—The portion of the window where the curve starts that goes to the tip and creates the curve.

Tip Opening—The actual opening measured from the mouthpiece table to the distance away from the tip rail opening. This is usually measured in thousandths of an inch in America and in millimeters in other countries.

Internal Mouthpiece Nomenclature:

Bore—The bore takes up much of the bottom of the mouthpiece from the bottom of the window. The top of the bore is the crown, and the exit of the bore is at the bottom of the mouthpiece.

Baffle—The surface opposite the window. This area controls brightness and darkness, and the ease of blowing, depending on how it's designed or modified. The closer the baffle is to the reed, the more brightness there is in the tone.

Chamber—The chamber is the area in front of the baffle and down to the bore area. The chamber has the biggest effect on tonal color and freedom, based on the proportions of the internal parts around it.

Sidewalls—To the sides of the chamber are the sidewalls and the width of the sidewalls becomes important. The shape of the sidewalls is very important in tone color and ease of playing.

Baffle Tip—The area about 1/8 of an inch from the tip on the mouthpiece. Some mouthpiece designs have what is called a *rollover* in this area, which helps the air through the mouthpiece, somewhat like an airplane wing.

Ramp—The area right underneath the table, inside the mouthpiece, where the window ends.

HOW TO SELECT A MOUTHPIECE

If you know, let the mouthpiece maker know what you are looking for. Play some music so the maker can hear you and discern any problems your setup may have. Let the maker know the size of reeds you are comfortable with. That will narrow down the mouthpiece search.

No matter how many times I have asked a musician before they come to my shop to have a selection of reeds in different sizes that play well to use in trying out a mouthpiece, almost 100% of the time they don't do it—and end up looking for a mouthpiece similar to what they have. What's the point of that?

It's good to have new reeds of various strengths that you have played briefly but are not yet married to your mouthpiece.

One thing is certain, many mouthpieces are quickly fixed by simply flattening the table.

Remember, that if you are looking for a new mouthpiece, you most likely are not completely happy with the mouthpiece you have, so keep an open mind. Be willing to learn how to play a new mouthpiece that you think is good. If a mouthpiece is close to what you want and has good qualities, you can get used to it.

Remember that the mouthpiece should function as a tool to make your job easier. Your concept will determine your sound and your equipment will help you or impede you from getting the sound you hear in your head.

Remember too, you are likely to sound like you already do unless you buy a somewhat different mouthpiece, so in selecting a mouthpiece, select one that makes it easier to fulfill your concept. Or, if you want to change your concept, buy a radically different mouthpiece, and learn to play it. Of course, this should probably be done with some guidance.

My background is classical, show work, celebrity accompaniment, jazz, and rock and roll, so I generally take three or four sax mouthpieces to a job where I don't know what to expect, so I can use the mouthpiece that will make the job easier for me. On clarinet, I take two mouthpieces, one on the classical side, and one more for jazz/pop/Broadway and microphone needs.

It's also important in selecting a mouthpiece to know what

acoustics you are working in. You could be in a carpeted pit, a concert hall, outside, a large motion picture studio, or a small home recording studio. Are you playing with a large group or a small ensemble or even putting a solo track on a pre-existing recording?

The correct mouthpiece can make any of these easier.

When selecting a mouthpiece, don't play all your fantastic excerpts or licks. Play slowly and listen to the mouthpiece and feel the response. Check the intonation of octaves, fifths, and fourths. Also make sure the mouthpieces tune to A=440, or whatever pitch those you play with use.

Only then, play an excerpt or your favorite lick to see if it feels good.

Mouthpiece makers have heard many solo concerts and are not really that interested in the technique of the musician except for listening to how the new mouthpiece can help the client.

Don't worry about facing numbers or openings or anything else. Just play the mouthpiece and listen and feel.

It's not a numbers game; it's a comfort game. A mouthpiece can have basically the numbers of the one that you covet and still not play the same.

No two mouthpieces play exactly the same!

Nothing drives a mouthpiece expert more bonkers than a client coming in and dictating a facing or adjustment when the whole mouthpiece needs to be considered. Each modification, even by a thousandth of an inch, affects every other measurement on the mouthpiece. A mouthpiece that plays well is a sum of *all of its parts,* and not just one measurement.

Some companies with the biggest names—ones that sell the most products on the market—don't necessarily make the best mouthpieces.

Buy the mouthpiece and not the name.

If you are studying with a teacher, and they suggest the same mouthpiece that they use, remember that the one you buy will not be exactly the same, most likely similar, but not the same. Ask to try your teacher's mouthpiece, reed, and ligature set-up, so you have something to compare to. Also, remember that your teacher's mouthpiece may be many years old and the company that made it may have altered the design.

There are many mouthpiece craftsmen who make good custom mouthpieces and there is probably one near you. Look on the web and ask around. If there is not one near you, it's best to take your vacation time and spend a day at the mouthpiece maker's shop.

It's much better if the client can come to the mouthpiece craftsman so the mouthpiece maker can see how you play. With mail order, you get the mouthpiece the maker imagines you want.

A mouthpiece should be tried on the instrument it's going to be used on, as each mouthpiece plays differently on every instrument.

You also need to consider mouthpiece patches when trying a mouthpiece, as they change the sound you hear in your head, and they change the opening of your mouth. I am an advocate of mouthpiece patches; however, there are many thicknesses, shapes, and brands of patches. If you know your preference, always use your preferred mouthpiece patch when trying a mouthpiece. If you don't use a mouthpiece patch, and the mouthpiece you are trying has a patch on it, take it off. Many times, this will make the difference in whether you like a mouthpiece or not. It's a small change, but in mouthpiece selection, small changes are significant.

Remember that terms like bright, dark, centered, big, free blowing, and a sound with a ping are all arbitrary and don't mean the same thing to any two people. Describing a sound really does not take you very far. You need to find a mouthpiece that sounds and feels like you want it to, and it's best to use descriptions in only the most general terms.

It's the craftsman's job not to moralize about "the correct sound," but to provide the performer with the mouthpiece that is what the client is looking for. That is, *if* the client even knows.

So, to review, mouthpieces are basically about your needs and making your practice and performance easier.

Many musicians are using aftermarket products. Specialists in particular aspects of instrument production are creating new and superior products all the time. Keep your eyes open for mouthpieces, ligatures, barrels, bells, and whatever new instrument concept is out there. The more you know the better you play.

General Thoughts on Success in Music

I would like to just give you a few thoughts on success in becoming a musician. In another article, I will go more deeply into my thoughts on what is required to become a success as a musician and in the music business.

Find the best private teacher in your area. This is worth some research. A good teacher will guide you and make learning easier. Be honest with the teacher about your practice habits and your goal with music.

Experience translates into value.

My first teacher was Johnny the Barber. Even though he was a very nice man, I probably could have found a better teacher to start with. Johnny just happened to teach at the local music store a couple of evenings a week.

Success is predicated on a regular study schedule. It's best to practice at the same time every day if you can. Some people love to practice. If you are not one of those people, you have to train yourself to enjoy practicing. Practicing needs to become a habit, or better yet, a ritual.

A casual approach gives casual results.

To do that, start by taking out your instrument as soon as you walk into the house and put it on an instrument stand. Put the stand and instrument in a conspicuous place where you see it as you walk by. If you feel like giving it a toot, go ahead and do it. If not, practice at the time you have selected.

Start slowly. Just practice one minute a day. You will most likely find yourself practicing a little more than the time you have allotted. That's good.

Add five minutes the next week—and build in that manner. You can always go back to one minute a day. That is the minimum.

Develop a concept of sound and style through listening to the radio, CD/audio devices, and live performances.

Make a point to attend live performances. This not only helps your concept, it helps you know what is expected of you when you perform and it's more fun and social than being under the headphones.

Listening is as important as practicing.

Think of an English teacher who does not read books. How could they ever have a concept of English, or the use of the language, as used by others? The same is true in music. Your experience in listening will help determine your concept.

Your concept is your tone and approach to the instrument, so take the time to listen. Listening is as important as practicing.

#10

The Changing Paradigm of Music

We are in a musical Renaissance like has never been known before. There are more virtuoso musicians in every genre of music than even existed in the European Renaissance of the 14th to 17th century. The rebirth is now, and it has brought many changes.

You have the love and passion to be a musician at some level. Keep your passion and practice every day so that passion can grow. The better you get, the better musicians you will play with and the more fun it will be. It's normal from time to time to consider quitting music. Never quit your instrument or your commitment to music on a whim. However, keep in mind that you may have to adapt to the new paradigms of music.

50 YEARS OF MUSIC IN THE UNITED STATES
(Some generalizations)

THEN	NOW
Mostly all union jobs	Mostly non-union jobs
Orchestras on every TV show	Live musicians on almost no TV Shows
Network TV	Network, Cable, Streaming, Satellite, etc.
Television broadcast drama, music and entertainment, news, sports, and game shows.	Call in, chat show, docudrama, documentary, docusoap, soap, fly on the wall, religion stations, infomercials, info-entertainment, magazine, mini-series, sitcom, tabloid, simulcasts and many more including the programming from 50 years ago
Professional Talent	Reality shows, talk shows, product sales shows
People went to clubs with a very active music scene	People stay home and there is very little club music.
No computers	Computers
Commercial composers composed for musicians	Commercial composers compose outstanding sounds on the computer, replacing musicians (*ok, not every time*) with a huge selection of instrument libraries
My first two vinyl records were analog	My last two CDs were digital and now available as downloads
My vinyl records sold in music shops and at concerts	My music sells on the Internet and can be segmentally purchased by track
My records were edited from 2-inch with a razor blade	My CDs are edited with a mouse and computer program
Composers wrote on paper	Composers compose & program using computers, apply quantizing, and the excellent composers even add feeling with time shifting
Entertainers had 28 piece minimum for local orchestras on most concert and show jobs	Entertainers come self-contained or use only 5 to 10 local musicians

THEN	NOW
Broadway pits had 18 to 28 local musicians	Broadway pits have 2 to 10 local musicians and bring 3 synths to fill out the orchestra. New shows are written for fewer musicians.
The majority of qualified musicians worked	There are many qualified musicians and many fewer jobs, so many extremely qualified musicians have no chance.
Music education was mostly classical	Most schools have classical, jazz, and pop music programs
There was AM/FM radio and Ham Radio	There are AM, FM, Satellite, HD, Internet, HAM, college non-profit, and community radio; and those just the ones I know of.
Symphony orchestras flourished, both in both big cities and small towns	Most orchestras struggle, some of the top 10 orchestras in the USA have declared some form of bankruptcy, orchestras ask musicians to accept lower salaries, the orchestras in many small towns are disappearing
Columbia Artists Community Concerts	Defunct
DJs on The Radio	DJs at your wedding *(all that money and no band)*

I could go on, however, with how the music business and the opportunity to play music is changing. Musicians are not just instrumentalists anymore, except when they can perform by playing alone, or with an established symphony or group. Those opportunities are also diminishing.

Though the music business is cyclical, it seems that as time goes on, it will become more difficult for musicians to make a living in the live music environment. Perhaps this forced requirement to know more about how music is made will make many dedicated instrumentalists and vocalists into better musicians, with new skills learned along the way.

These days, having at least a cursory understanding of computers and the way they can be used to create music, will be essential to becoming a successful musician. However, reading music and understanding the nuance of live performance will remain essential.

The more flexibility you have as a performer and the more things you can do related to music, the better chance you will have to succeed in the future and stay with our friend—music.

Many musicians I know write music (a great opportunity for musical growth) and own their recording or midi studio (another great opportunity) or both. Jokingly they are called *midiots*.

The question is, how good are you at these computer programs: Digital Performer, Logic, Sibelius, Encore, Finale, Pro Tools, etc.? How good are you at writing music, copying music, recording, repairing computers, updating music software, or helping composers that need help with these programs?

One of the best musicians I have ever met, and who is at the top of his career, also has a woodwind specialty shop, where he sells instruments and accessories and teaches.

Teaching is another great music-related opportunity, as through teaching we reinforce and re-evaluate what we do to play and make changes as necessary. We also learn patience **Be in the right place at the right time.** and the tactics to help people grow. Private teaching makes us better players. It's a good living too, especially when teaching from of your home or a studio you may rent.

Any music-related sideline is a good thing to know. Knowledge is success.

Learning to compose on a computer, or on paper, is a strong addition to any musician's musical worth.

If you live in a place where there is no concert band, no chamber music, no jazz, no R&R, or no orchestra, start a group of some sort. Most successful musicians are self-starters at some level.

Also, the best working musicians are good businesspeople and good politicians. Life is largely business and politics, and that translates to having lots of good friends. The best way to have a good friend is to be a good friend. That's how your name and your friend's names get circulated.

Let's be clear. I am not asking you to reconsider music or the music business.

I am asking you to grow to encompass more of music, and for those professionals reading this, to grow to be able to have broader knowledge about the trends in the business. Music and the music business will always be here, but most likely not like it was last year, five years ago, ten years ago, twenty years ago, fifty years ago, or a hundred years ago.

Turn frustration into fascination.

Constant growth is required.

Get better at your specialty while embracing new music-related horizons. Think of ways you can grow and what music-related fields you are interested in that will or can add to your worth and enjoyment.

Below is another tidbit about music streaming and what that brings to musicians. David is a pop musician; however, his articles are worth thinking about for musicians in any genre. By going to the website below, you can read many other articles about our business (you must read to the bottom of each article to get the next link).

https://davidbyrne.com/how-will-the-wolf-survive-can-musicians-make-a-living-in-the-streaming-era

Laws of Success

I don't know about you, but when I was in school, no one ever talked about money. How to get it, how to keep it, when to spend it, and what to spend it on, were never mentioned. To me, this is a real void in the education system, and I hope all your music teachers will talk with their administration to see that all students, not just music students, learn what to expect financially in the real world.

I was lucky, as the Musicians Union pension system worked well for most of my career. While that is not true now, it was for most of my vesting time. This, along with Social Security, investments that I started making when I was 55, and a couple of side businesses, has left me very comfortable. And then there is the Motion Picture Special Payments Fund. I would never have been successful without the Union pension or Special Payments Fund, as I had no idea about money until I learned about it for myself as I saw retirement age coming faster than I planned.

HOW ABOUT YOU?

What's *your plan* for having a financial cushion during your working years that will extend into your retirement? Remember, it's not only the money you make but also **the money you keep and make grow** that can give you a peaceful retirement, free of financial worries.

One of the first major books on the subject of personal success was *The Law of Success* by Napoleon Hill. It was the financial bible that every business major read. There are now hundreds of books telling you how to be successful. My suggestion is that you read *The Law of Success*. It's available in hardcover, paperback, Kindle, and as an audiobook. Hill also wrote *Think and Grow Rich*, his most popular book. I suggest you read that book also.

Keep in mind that these books were written in the 1930s, so you will have to adjust your reading with his references to life at the time and substitute your own examples. However, the lessons stand as he teaches them. You may not use all of them, but if you don't read at least one of these books, you will be doing yourself a disservice.

SELF PROMOTION

So, what is important on a daily basis? How do you promote yourself?

1. Remember that everyone you meet, rehearse with, or work with, whether more proficient than you or not as proficient, should be treated with respect for trying to keep up in the time-consuming art and business of music. **Be a good sincere friend to everyone. Be a good listener. Be kind to those people who you don't feel comfortable with as you don't know what demons they were taught.**

2. **Have a business card.** That sounds corny these days. What a business card does for you is make a quick transfer of contact information possible. Remember a business card is two-sided, so if the front is for the contact information you want to give out, the back might be a good place to put your website address or other information you might feel to be important. When you put a phone number on the card, try to make it your permanent phone number for life. Having your own Internet domain is also important, as phone numbers can change, but the Internet is *forever*. People who want to contact you will appreciate your reliability. Know when

it's appropriate to present your business card. Buy a small number of cards—say 300—as you will want to change them from time to time. The formality of always exchanging cards as the proper thing to do when meeting someone is no longer necessarily appropriate, but why not be prepared?

So, what if you don't have a business card? *Then it's... I'll find a pen... do you have some paper... just tell me your email address and I will remember it,... etc.* None of these options work. When you give someone your card, you make them responsible for it. They may immediately throw it away, or they may keep it, perhaps throw it in their card file/box as an archive. I go through my card file about once a year, when I give my desk drawers a good cleaning and only throw the cards away of those who I don't remember. At a certain point, the cards I keep go into my database for permanent storage. The point is, you give someone a piece of paper with your information that they then become responsible for.

3. **A CD or DVD is the new business card.** With a CD or DVD, people can hear or see what you do. With the inexpensive and excellent digital recorders available, there is no reason even a student can't have a good recording of some sort. For students, it's good to record a music track every year so you can monitor your musical growth, and when you think you are good enough, you can make a short CD and give it to friends, relatives, and people who might be able to help your musical growth. Record something you can sound good on, even if it is *Mary Had a Little Lamb*, for beginners. Get used to recording and being in front of a camera. It's the immediate future of our industry. For a professional, it's *imperative* you have a CD or DVD as a business card.

4. **Social Media.** This is the best way to reach countless new contacts. Be careful though, about what you post, and the way you post it. You can share your recorded tracks with others who may be looking for someone to perform with or may be able to help you sell your tracks. You will gradually meet many people who

have similar interests to yours. But, it's important not to be provocative in public forums.

Let me give you an example: If you post that you went to a wild party, that's great for the people who are party people, but for those who are not, they will see you in a negative light, which is not good for your career. So be conservative in posts and keep your more colorful actions for emails or communication with those friends who think like you do (your private list). Again, remember that the Internet is *forever*.

Know how people want to communicate, so you can converse with them on a level they are comfortable with. Does the person you are talking to prefer snail mail, email, telephone, cellular phone, texting, Skype, or instant messaging from their main computer, etc.? Some people even like to talk over dinner or a cup of coffee, I know that's hard to believe. **Make the person at the other end comfortable, and communicate at their preferred technical level.**

5. **Be Seen.** "Out of sight, out of mind" was the old saying, and it holds true today. Go to concerts, recitals, clubs, and wherever else music is being played. Especially if you know the musicians. If the musicians are new to you, you have the easy opportunity to go up and introduce yourself and tell them how much you enjoyed the music and their playing.

   Play in as many groups as you can. The people you meet when you are young will keep coming back into your life. Take auditions and attend and **Out of sight, Out of mind.** play at contests and master classes. Even if you don't get the reward, the "powers that be" get to know you, and might tell someone else about you. People usually don't think far in advance about their needs if they run a group of some kind. They look for a musician when they need a musician, so if you have the luck to be around when they need someone, you just might get a place to play. It has happened to me, so I know it works. Also, people like to work and perform with people they are comfortable with, so once you are in a group, if you are a good friend, and play well enough, chances are you will be with that group for a very long time. Also give concerts/recitals/soirées. Invite your family, friends, and those who you would like to hear you.

6. **Advertise and promote your concerts, your CDs and DVDs.** Musicians need to be self-starters to be successful unless they are musical geniuses of some sort. Depending on your age, promotion can be very different. If you are young, just putting a flyer in the band/orchestra room, the choir room and around campus, and inviting your relatives might be enough. Mail the fliers to your relatives and friends. If you are a professional, make sure you advertise on social media, in newspapers, and on media sources. You might even call a media outlet and arrange an interview to discuss your concert. How about a mailing list? If you start when you are young and spend about an hour a week keeping your list up to date, and adding new members, you can get thousands of people on your list before you know it. Just like this article was sent to my mailing list. Don't be shy about asking people to join your list.

7. **Don't put all your eggs in one basket**. If you are training to be a symphonic clarinetist, it doesn't hurt to play the sax well enough to play "Romeo and Juliet" or "Pictures" at an Exhibition. It also doesn't hurt to play sax if a pop act comes to play with your orchestra. You might just keep the work for the night by being able to play sax. Many full-time time musicians teach. The best way to learn is to teach, and at the same time you are giving back to your art just like someone did for you. The pocket change doesn't hurt either. You get the idea. A little flexibility and interest in other things might make you a better musician.

8. **Dress Appropriately**. Whether the dress code for your group is a tuxedo, suit, blazer, jeans and a t-shirt, black pants and a white shirt, or whatever, LOOK GOOD. If it's cool to have long hair, have good-looking long hair. If you shave your head, make sure

it's freshly shaved. If you have a beard, make sure it's at least semi-trimmed. Look like you are ready to go to the event. Most musicians hate the thought of being in "show business"—however, whether you're simply playing in front of someone, even in a recording studio, everyone looks at you. You don't have to try and out-dress anyone, but you do need to look presentable. Remember that everyone you meet might be able to help you in some way and looking ready always helps. Whether or not you like it, even though it should not be that way, people do evaluate you partly on your looks as part of your total package.

I have given you some ideas to help ensure your success. These are only some of the tools. Think about it. You don't need to make a living in music. Most likely, unless you are really motivated and have no other choice, you should not count on making a living in music. Make it fun.

> *Life's greatest inconsistency is the fact*
> *that most of what we believe is not true.*
> **—Napoleon Hill**

If you choose to make a living in music, there is some business involved. Pay attention to the business that you are in.

SAVE YOUR MONEY !!!

Unless you are born into money, it drops from the sky, or you live in a monastery, money, skills in how to use money, and how to keep money are important to develop.

> **Save Your Money!**
> **Invest Your Money!**
> **Protect Your Money!**

What Do You Own?

Let's start with a C major scale:

Do we need to think of the names of the notes to play it, or do we just see the notes, realize it's a C major scale, and play them without any further thought process? Do we play it one octave at a time, or two octaves, or throughout the range of the instrument, up and down ending on the tonic C? Can we manipulate the scale? That is, play it in thirds and fourths, etc.? Have we played all the simple childhood tunes available to this one scale alone? Do we know where to breathe to make the scale sound the best?

Do we think of the scale in quarter notes, eighth notes, or sixteenth notes, etc., and why? Is it because of our concept or the phrasing that the scale requires a certain feeling? To own the scale, the accents must be appropriate for the speed and style of the music being played.

Answering "Yes" to those questions means you probably *own* the C Major Scale. So, then the next question becomes, "Can we do all this in all the keys on our instrument?"

> *Here is an experiment:* Start the C major scale and breathe after the first note and then finish the scale. Do the same breathing after the 2nd note, and continue on in the same manner, breathing after each note in the scale. It becomes obvious which breathing works best.

Breathing then becomes a huge part of phrasing. Where we breathe is like a comma in a sentence. Part of *owning* a phrase is knowing where to breathe.

Next Logical Question of Ownership

Do we know the F# major scale (or any other major scale) as well as we know the C major scale? There's a perception that keys with more sharps or flats are more difficult, but in reality, they're just different, and something new to learn. Take the time to learn them...to OWN them...just like we did the C major scale.

These are just a few ideas for us to learn to *own* the scale instead of just *kind of knowing it*. Once we own it, we can make a simple scale sound like a piece of music that someone would enjoy listening to.

LIFE AFTER THE MAJORS

Then there are all the other scales that seem more important to jazz and improvising musicians because they are composing spontaneously and require a bit more harmonic knowledge. It's important, though, that we don't think that this knowledge is only important for improvisers. Harmonic knowledge is important for every musician, including those who only read music.

For the improviser, do we know the F#7 (#5 #9) as well as the C7, or do we freeze and turn on the internal dialogue when approaching this chord? Do we *own* the (#5 #9) chord even in F#?

So here we have it. The answer. Starting with just a major scale.

Own it.

What's next?

Learn to own something else in music. It's a never-ending journey.

Do we understand the meaning of each scale? Bach and Glen Gould did.

Possibly the best music lesson in my life was following the Urtext score to Glen Gould's 1955 recording of the *Goldberg Variations* by J.S. Bach.

At first, I watched and listened to one line of the two to four parts he would be playing. I listened for the phrasing, as he massaged the line, moving forward and backward, ever so subtly, and for the finger pressure of each note, amazed that his little finger could play with the same strength and nuance as his thumb, or first finger could. Then I would follow another line.

After that, I would try to follow two lines at once and then all the musical lines. I did this with each movement until I

Sing music, even instrumental music.

could understand how he took the notes off the paper and made it music. He owned the music and not just the technique. Even though the technique was difficult to learn, he kept practicing it until it was a song in his body and mind.

I strongly suggest you buy an Urtext piano part to the *Goldberg Variations* along with Glen's first 1955 recording and take the time to hear the music come off the page. Take your time. It's a big journey. It was one of the best educational experiences in my life on phrasing and music, transcending the written page. Now there are many fantastic versions of the *Goldberg Variations*; you will enjoy each recording in a different way. I love András Schiff and all his recordings as of this writing. Also listen to the sound of each piano. However, because Bach has a lot of notes, sometimes a really ringing piano will get in the way of the stream of notes.

Alas, nothing is always perfect, even if we own it. However, isn't it nice to know we have something personal in our repertoire even if it's a child's tune that we own? The more we own the more we become.

#13

Diaries

I have talked about keeping a diary before. If you have not started one yet, please do it now. This is a great way for us to remember powerful quotes that can shape our life, resolve many of our conflicts, and show shortcuts to our paths.

It's important to go to a good source and get a journal with a hard-cover and firm paper, as these diaries will serve us for the rest of our lives, to be updated and reviewed at regular intervals.

In addition to collecting thoughts from great thinkers, we can add our own thoughts and daily insights. So, we can review our own thinking as time goes by.

These are thoughts, not just about music, but about success in life, or joy, which of course makes music easier. These quotes are a just few from my several full diaries.

Find your own quotes and write them down.

Take your time, as you make entries to your diary, and as you review your diary, so you can soak in the true meanings of the writings.

Look up any words that are not completely understood. Here is an example:

Success is largely a matter of tactful and
harmonious negotiation with other people.
——Napoleon Hill, The Law of Success

There should be a period of time during each practice session when we perform. Invite some friends or family into your practice room and play a passage or a page of something, or pretend there is a conductor on the other side of the door with a $90K job waiting for you based on your performance ... or, simply turn your tape recorder on, and perform for the microphone. What I am trying to indicate is that each day should contain some amount of performing. You should engage in the deliberate act of storytelling each day you practice. Don't only gather information when you practice, spend time imparting it. This is important!
—Arnold Jacobs
Tuba, Chicago Symphony

In my entire career I sang the way I wanted six times. The rest of the time I did the best I could.
—Beverly Sills

If you hang out at the barbershop long enough, sooner or later you're going to get a haircut.
—Denzel Washington

The magic of any art is not only in its technique, but in its authenticity. Truth in its rawest form is what resonates most powerfully.
—Alicia Keys

#14

Colleagues in the Music Business

We have many people in our business who help us do our job; librettists, composers, orchestrators / arrangers, copyists, conductors, librarians, A&R representatives, along with their record companies and distributors, agents, managers, music licensing companies, recording engineers, sound engineers, lighting and staging professionals, cartage companies, radio stations, computer resources and streaming music, music schools, private music teachers, music and instrument suppliers, boutique music shops, repair technicians, concert venues, unions, critics, those who clean up after our performance, and those sitting next to us... to name few.

... *Whew*

It's important that we show respect to everyone who helps us do our job.

I would like to explain in this, and in subsequent e-broadcasts, the importance of our friends and colleagues—and what they do to help make us sound good *(or bad)*.

For a moment we should consider the 10% rule that says that only 10% of the people in any discipline or job own what they are doing. The rest are in some state of treading water or trying to get better. It sounds ruthless; however, if I were to have surgery, I would like a doctor that's in the top 10% of doctors worldwide. Nothing is perfect, but minimizing risk is a primary consideration. In the same way, it's much more rewarding to play a piece of music where the composer understands what you do and writes to the strength of your instrument or voice.

THE COMPOSER

The first person in the line of music creation is the composer—the person that stares at the blank page before writing a note.

I would like to start with librettists, and songwriters, as they face the same dilemma as the full-blown symphonic composer. *They start with a blank page or computer screen.* Think about that for a moment… With the vastness of music and styles available, they face nothing but that blank page.

Their creativity must come from within their mind, with the tools they have or may not have. It's a bit easier, I would think, to write words, as we all know our language to some extent, and have some idea of whether or not the words we put together feel good. However, great librettists can tell a sad, funny, profound, or happy story with syntax and a mastery of the language that few of us possess.

There are librettists who write pop music or jazz music, others write show music, opera, and a variety of other styles. They may or may not know music at all. For those that can't write their own music and put it on paper or computer, there is the composer as a collaborator.

The composer takes the blank page … *think about that again … a blank page or computer screen* … along with the words the librettist gives them, and either adds the music or puts the music to paper that the songwriter may not be able to transfer there. *(Think of a guitarist-singer who can play and sing his tune but can't read music.)*

I am talking now about pop music and the way music and words get put together. Though it's only the seed of a final product, and perhaps not the arrangement that is required to make a final product, the wordsmith and the pop composer must come up with a viable product that pleases many people. That includes the audience as well as all the intermediary people that get it to the audience, which is no small feat. The point is that something must be done. A band or the writers must learn to play the music, or it must be arranged for a particular number of musicians to make it come to fruition.

Next, I want to talk about the composers of original classical, film, Broadway, jazz, opera, and art music in general. *The blank page is getting more profound.*

A composer starts with a blank page . . . *think carefully about that.* Let's start again with that blank page. I have to say that I have made a living in the music business my whole life and have never faced a blank page with the intent of writing a major piece of music or even a jingle. I did write and record a blues tune, and that was hard enough. It dumbfounds me to think about the musical mountain that composers must encounter.

They must face every technique of music they own, plus every technique they *wished* they owned, or must learn, to reach the summit of a finished piece of music. A *composition* if you will.

They are judged by almost everyone in their pursuit to create. Though they mostly judge themselves and can doubt themselves, many others judge them. We, as musicians judge them, the audience judges them, and yes even the critics judge them. Therein lies the folly, as everyone is a critic, but usually a critic limited by their own musical vocabulary.

As musicians, we have all played compositions we thought to be inferior or worthless, usually based on the difficulty (*impossibility, to be more precise*) posed to our particular instrument. In addition, there is the overall validity of the work. Of course, this all changes as time changes. Bach was not all that accepted by the public in his own time either. However, there are plainly inferior pieces of music, it must be said, and that's what makes the great pieces *truly great.*

Like most musicians, composers (*geniuses not included*) grow as they mature and have more technique and sophistication. The composers who seem to be the most musically friendly to musicians though, are the ones who got an early start on their studies—not just harmonic and rhythmic studies, but studies about the essence of each instrument they write for. Surely, *The Rite of Spring* expanded the range for the bassoon, but for good use, and while extremely difficult, it was perfect to describe the story.

Many times, composers write difficult instrumental parts for no reason except not knowing what an instrument can do *(theory or lack of theory, with no knowledge of the instruments they write for)*. It's important for the composer to *appropriately* challenge the player with something that is quite playable even if a lot of practice is necessary. On the other hand, if the part can be made easier, and have the same effect, the composer should consider this option first. *(Oh, please don't make me practice.)*

Another dilemma is the composer who writes on the synthesizer and "steps-in" the notes—and then expects the musician to play it back at a tempo that's unrealistic for their instrument.

Composers of classical music almost always write the original music from the blank page and orchestrate the piece of music too. So, a composer of this type is also their own orchestrator. They may sketch musical lines and chords, but ultimately, they are responsible for every note to be copied into individual parts for musicians.

With the help of computers, today's composers can hear a fairly accurate rendition of their composition. Many composers today write at the piano, or by musical rules or sounds in their head. Imagine the thrill of hearing your composition for the first time. It can be exhilarating, embarrassing, or any other adjective you want to use.

Of course, the more skilled the composer is, the more often they are satisfied with the outcome of their creative adventure. The ability to communicate the composer's intentions to the musicians is very important at this point, as any first playing is a balancing act just to bring the music to fruition.

Many music enthusiasts have looked down on the film composer as being less than a "serious" composer. I'm talking now about the film composer who actually writes all their own music. But what must be remembered is *that a media composer is a serious composer with a larger sound and style palette, at their fingertips.* This is not to be dismissed lightly.

Think about what has been done in creating something from nothing, so you as an instrumentalist or vocalist can perform a composition by others with respect and understanding of their ability. It's an important part of the marriage of music and all its participants.

Even improvisers work from some sort of a framework, whether it be from a lead sheet or an arrangement that a composer or arranger has created from that blank sheet of paper. . . . It all starts from a blank piece of paper!

I urge all musicians to ask a composer to compose for them to increase the literature, for the sake of us all. Some composers will want remuneration for their work, and the ones who are financially able or happen to be a friend of yours will be happy to do it for the sake of our art.

I have commissioned many compositions, and whether they were recorded, as many were, or played for a concert, it was always a rewarding situation for the composer, musician, and the public alike.

A writer is like a tuning fork:
We respond when we're struck by something. The thing
is to pay attention, to be ready for radical empathy. If we
empty ourselves of ourselves we'll be able to vibrate in
synchrony with something deep and powerful. If we're
lucky we'll transmit a strong pure note, one that isn't
ours, but which passes through us. If we're lucky, it will
be a note that reverberates and expands, one that other
people will hear and understand.
— Roxana Robinson

#15

Orchestrators, Arrangers and Copyists/Publishers

In our previous ezine, dedicated to those whom we work with and who help us do our jobs in music, we talked about composers. To continue, in this broadcast, we will talk about arrangers, orchestrators, and copyists/publishers.

ORCHESTRATORS AND ARRANGERS

Make no mistake about it. Arrangers and orchestrators, at times, are also called upon to be composers, in that when they receive a score, there's no telling how finished it will be. They may receive anything from a sketch to a nearly finished product.

To me, the one significant difference between an orchestrator and arranger is that an orchestrator usually works in the visual media (film, TV, etc.), and an arranger generally works in the recording and live arenas (CDs and live shows, usually for a singer, a band, or an "act").

These days, orchestrators usually know exactly what instruments they are writing for. They have a budget and a designated instrumentation. This rarely changes.

With dwindling budgets in performance venues, arrangers know that at some point their music might be cut down by a certain number of instruments to reach those budgets.

Many times, a conductor, administrator, agent, on anyone else in the chain, could decide to cut the orchestra down from 21 to 18, or 15, or 10, or even 6, for example.

Those who cut down orchestras, and thus orchestrations, must realize that an arranger can only go so far in planning to have an arrangement work with people cut from an orchestra without writing a new arrangement. The other option is to have the altered arrangement sound weak, to the detriment of everyone except the producer who is saving the money and putting it in their pocket.

Take a five-note chord and take two notes out. Now listen to how it sounds. You like?

Think of hearing an orchestration on the big screen, a full-length picture—*Ratatouille, Star Wars, Room with a View, Psycho, Africa,* and many other classics of movie music.

Think of the thrill of hearing a horn arrangement for Aretha Franklin, Tower of Power, or your string arrangement for Barbara Streisand, Tony Bennett, Ray Charles, Johnny Mathis, Natalie Cole, or any number or the great singers who still use a band and string sections.

This is a gift from our friends, the orchestrators and arrangers. Great Music!

COPYISTS / PUBLISHERS

Copyists can receive a "score" in any condition these days, from completely finished and written out, to an mp3 file that needs to be deciphered. These are the people who save us time and money with products that have very few if any mistakes. Copying mistakes takes us time to correct. Time is at a premium every time musicians get together in this busy world.

Publishers get music that is generally ready to print, or can choose to publish the copyists' work as originally generated. They too, have the responsibility of providing music with no mistakes, or each performer who plays their music must find and fix that mistake. They have a very high average. My only problem with publishers over the years is that, in order to save every ounce of paper, they will usually not make a page turn at a long rest, lest they waste paper. This leaves the performer to have to photocopy the piece or cut it up so page turns can be made more easily.

Integrity

Honor, decency, righteousness, principled, uprightness, scrupulousness, rectitude, morality, character, nobility, and pride are all dictionary synonyms for the word *integrity*.

A friend of mine—a tax professional and former insurance salesman, owner of a carpet mill, furniture store, and childcare center, and CFO of two jingle companies—told me the other day, in discussing *integrity*, that there is no honor in business. He said that honor in business is the *exception*, rather than the *rule*.

He taught me a lesson that I had not fully understood during my career in the music business.

No one is perfect, and I have failed from time to time, especially in my earlier years when I wanted to be a musician so badly that I was willing to give up the idea of the integrity that I was taught as a child just so I could be in the music business and stay in it.

The problem was that it didn't make me feel very good.

At some point early on, I lost my integrity, I lost myself—and that forced me to change, and to strive to be a better person.

I have been through many things in my career. While working to become a virtuoso musician, I still had an interest in entrepreneurial endeavors. From my vantage point, I was always a little less successful in entrepreneurial endeavors than in musical endeavors. I wanted to make money—and lots of it; however, I could seldom sacrifice someone else to make a sale. In most cases, a successful salesman would make the sacrifice for the sake of the sale.

The truth is, the business of performing music is also an entrepreneurial job, mixed with the artistic aplomb that must always accompany it. The same goes for other music jobs, whether it be owning a music store, being a repairperson, running a performing arts center, or any of the myriad of other jobs related to music.

So, the question becomes: "How do we do our business and perform our music with integrity?"

Some people are lucky, and integrity just works for them, so it's an easy choice. Make no mistake though, "idealism does not go unpunished," and even those who find it easy to have honor will experience this.

Like telling the truth: So we are never caught in a lie, which ultimately becomes damaging to our image, it's just easier not to lie and keep a little bit of our integrity intact. Though others can get away with lying, if not by word but by action, I think many of us feel a twinge of some sort when we fail to honor our own integrity.

> *Tell a lie once and all your*
> *truths become questionable.*
> —Terri Labunski

What makes it so difficult and confusing? The fact that *our* truth is not always the truth of others.

We *can* have integrity within the confines of our own limitations while realizing that there will always be people with greater or lesser skills and experience than ourselves. Saying negative things about any comrade in music is mostly a reflection on ourselves, not on them. We can always make great and valid music within our own limits.

> *Honor is a person's gift they give to themselves.*
> —Tom Clancy

Money is transitory. Honor isn't.
—Tom Clancy

There are many personalities in life, and the fact is that each of us is unique. How our personality works with our integrity takes many years of trial and error. Hopefully, that's what childhood is for, but most of us take longer to learn these lessons. Some people never resolve how to pair their personality with integrity, thus creating their own kind of uneasiness.

It's amazing what you can accomplish
if you do not care who gets the credit.
—Harry S. Truman

Integrity means something different to every person on the planet, but I propose that it comes back to the first sentence of this dialogue.

So, let me just write it again:

Integrity is…honor, decency, righteousness, principles, uprightness, scrupulousness, rectitude, morality, character, nobility, and pride.

Those who stand for nothing,
fall for anything"
—Alexander Hamilton

Each time a man stands up for an ideal,
or acts to improve the lot of others,
or strikes out against injustice,
he sends forth a tiny ripple of hope…
—Robert F. Kennedy

Artists are people driven by the tension between
the desire to communicate and the desire to hide.
—D.W. Winnicot

#17

Concept

The dictionary says:

> Concept:(konsept) n.
> an idea, especially an abstract idea

Most students have no concept of jazz, classical, or ethnic music, except for their use in motion pictures and other media—where they are for the most part not aware of the music, because of all the dialogue and sound effects.

I don't think there is a need in this article to cite all the studies that show how music is important in the nurturing of the brain and creative thinking in all areas. Those ideas are an accepted truth.

So where does someone get a musical concept?

Generally, the concept comes from family, school, and private teachers, the environment, and from the student simply listening to something new without prejudice.

We are comfortable with what we know. Being confronted with new knowledge, feelings, and new experiences can be painful, as it may be in opposition to our normal concept.

Learning is a painful process.
—Jack Wheaton

Some people have never heard live instruments, a symphony, a jazz band, rock & roll, ethnic music or, in some instances, live music of any kind. The question then becomes how to present the importance of music to students and people of all ages. That takes time and effort.

Arranging to have live music in the schools by presenting musical groups is a start. So is a school music program (if it happens to exist, what with today's limited school budgets). In the case of beginning students, time is spent on just getting a sound out of the instrument and little time is given to the idea of listening to develop a concept. All the better reason, of course, to have a private instructor right from the beginning and music in the home.

The better the concept, the better the understanding of the available musical panorama.

It becomes the role of parents and teachers to improve their own concept of music and play that music in the home, and during rest breaks at school, thereby enhancing the gestalt, the concept, the understanding, and the enjoyment of the student.

Most youngsters listen to the music that's presented to them on pop music stations and use that music as the basis for social interaction. At about the age of 20–25, when people start the time-consuming duties of being an adult, they stop growing musically and hold on to the music of their youth for the rest of their lives. That becomes *their* "good" music. This usually limits what they can offer their offspring and is usually at odds with what the young person is listening to. This is repeated generation after generation.

Thankfully, and for the first time in the history of mankind, the current free media has every type of music one can imagine if one wants to take advantage of giving different types of music a chance. My suggestion to parents, teachers, and even youngsters, is to tune in to radio and new streaming stations, and even music stations on television, and gently try for a few minutes to listen to something that is new, just for the experience. If you find something you like, buy a CD, and learn to live that music.

WHAT IS GOOD MUSIC?

Defending "good" music, or the music each of us has accepted as our own, is a dead-end street. All music is "good." Gaining more musical understanding may affect our listening preferences, as we become more sophisticated listeners, but that certainly does not negate our favorites from youth.

Concepts are so important because we use them daily. They are our *constant filters*. They include what we eat and how much, if we are basically happy people or not, how we perceive ourselves and others, our religion, or lack of same. Other concepts include our idea of honesty, the use of money, the treatment of others, and virtually every action we take. We justify them all for the sake of our concept.

Are your concepts based on some sort of truth or just something you have been told and chosen to believe? It's an important distinction for growth in our lives.

A murderer usually kills because they think that the other person deserves it for some reason, not because they consider themselves to be a bad person doing a bad deed. An extreme concept gone wrong. Then again, I assume your concept does not include murder.

It's important for each of us to examine all our concepts from time to time, making sure that they are still valid and have not morphed into mistaken beliefs that we continue to hold.

As far as music is concerned, let's all agree to try to expand our concepts. It's worth a few minutes a day and may give us a little more understanding of ourselves and of the world.

Let's discuss for a moment, you as a music *student* or as a music *teacher*. After all, we are teachers and students all the time and with every action we take.

As a teacher, are you solely the product of *your* teacher? Are you passing on to your students only what your teacher taught you or adding concepts that you have learned through your own experiences?

As a student, are you playing on a mouthpiece, instrument, or reed that your teacher told you to use, even though it makes you uncomfortable? Does your teacher give you rigid concepts, or allow you to develop your own concepts, along with him/her? As a student, do you follow your teacher strictly, or do you use your own ideas to help develop *your* concept, and discuss these ideas with your teacher?

Your musical concept comes from listening, practicing, maturing, having a good instrument, reflection, environment, and many other factors. If one listens to only Dixieland music and practices only Dixieland music, they become a Dixieland musician. So, what happens if someone practices Dixieland, Classical and Ethnic music?

I was a dedicated student well into my early 30s, and at one point went to a new teacher who said to me, "You seem to have the same problems as I do, so why don't you just take some political lessons from all the leading teachers around and see if they can get you some work." That most likely, was the best lesson I ever had, despite many years of great private instructors. I'd had a student's concept!

We become what we do on a daily basis.

He "fired" me as a student at a time when I would have been only a student for the rest of my life. He made me responsible for learning on my own and basing my studies on what I heard. Everyone I heard or encountered became my teacher in some way.

Talk amongst your friends with your ideas on how to improve the concept of music in our schools, in our homes, and for ourselves. We might become better people because of it.

Practicing *for* Your Students

As teachers, we have all been advising students, demonstrating for students, showing students shortcuts, and teaching students how to practice. I would dare say we never practice *for* our students.

Recently, I took the opportunity to practice for one of my advanced students. I felt that he'd never really fully understood how to practice, no matter how I suggested he do it. I took a very difficult piece I'd been practicing for several months, but had not yet mastered, and let him see how I approached it.

I asked him to not talk during my practice session but to only listen and watch. In addition to working on the piece of music, a clarinet quintet by John Scott, I was also finishing up adjusting reeds that would work for the piece. So, at times, I would stop and make minor final adjustments to the reed so it would feel the most comfortable for that piece of music.

This was the first time I'd ever practiced in front of anyone except my own teachers.

My student was amazed and said he learned a lot. He was particularly interested to see that when I had even a minor mishap, I would go back and go over the passage several times very slowly, which my friend Gerry Schroeder calls *"tempo de learno."*

Of course, I had been suggesting this to him for years. As I gradually brought the phrase up to tempo and was able to play it, the student immediately understood not only the idea of seeing the music and hearing the phrase, finding the weak notes in the phrase, but he could also see and hear the finger memory being learned along with the nuance of the phrase *(which notes belong together)*. He also learned how quickly a phrase can be mastered when starting slow and increasing the speed and not just slopping over it and assuming it's good enough.

The student also understood the refinement of the reed and how the reed can actually make the piece easier by being balanced and voiced for ease of playing for the mouthpiece, instrument, and repertoire.

It made me think that I should practice for all of my students so they really understand how to do it.

Have you ever practiced *for* a student?

The bottom line is that I think it is important to practice something we really can't play well *for* our students during a lesson, *for the whole lesson*, occasionally, so they see and understand the intensity and commitment of practicing, and how much faster they can improve if they practice correctly.

I still live by the thought that it is not only how long a student *(or anyone for that matter)* practices, but it's the regularity with which they practice. With regularity, we can't help but practice more, as the act of practicing is interesting, and as one improves and it becomes easier to get better, the interest just normally increases.

I heard a quote not long ago and I don't remember who told it to me, but it goes like this (and I most likely paraphrase):

"Rehearsals are not for you to practice; they are the opportunity for you to hear what others have practiced."

That implies that one must come to band and orchestra rehearsals fully prepared, and to approach the ensemble as if the conductor may ask you to play the hardest section in the composition alone.

So, my student friends...know your part before you get to rehearsal, even if it's a community band, orchestra, or chamber ensemble and you are all doing it just for "fun." It's a lot more fun if everyone knows their part.

> *I've never known a musician who regretted being one.*
> *Whatever deceptions life may have in store for you,*
> *music itself is not going to let you down.*
> **—Virgil Thompson**

What to Teach a Beginning Woodwind Student

"FOR SCHOOL TEACHERS"
Part 1

I want to be clear with all public-school music teachers: I think you are all angels and personally I can't imagine a more difficult job. You are required to know a lot about music, the psychology of the students and their parents, and possess a ton of patience. And you can't dismiss the student if they aren't taking it seriously, as a private teacher can.

I am a woodwind specialist. I play and teach clarinet, saxophone, flute, and oboe, and know absolutely nothing about playing the bassoon. I know nothing of any of the other families of instruments, except that I perform with them, and understand some of their idiosyncrasies.

I usually have between one and four students at any time, and most are intermediate or advanced. This year, I have had the opportunity to teach a nine-year-old beginner on the sax, a high school music teacher on the clarinet, and a gentleman in his eighties, who came to me as an early intermediate clarinet student, and in just a year with a complete commitment, has become an advanced student with

169

surprising improvement. I also had one brilliant student on an oboe, something we get only every few years; someone who will have his choice of any job in the music business he desires, due to his intense interest and powerful study habits. He is now finishing his Doctoral program at Yale and it actually has improved his playing—an oddity for many doctorate recipients.

Student Level

As a music teacher in elementary or middle school, you are likely to encounter students of limited experience.

I want to discuss with you what to do when teaching a beginning student who comes to you the first day they pick up an instrument.

Unfortunately, with school budgets as they are, a beginning music student can have a math teacher with a music minor as their mentor, or, if they are more fortunate, they can get a music expert with a degree, or even better yet, they can get a teacher who is trained on their specific instrument or family of instruments.

School Music Teacher and Private Instructor—Do Students Need Both?

Let me start with the most obvious statement that I am sure you will agree with: "It's important, if not imperative, for the beginning student to have a private instructor."

If you are very lucky as a teacher, you will be able to talk parents into private lessons. You still will want to have occasional "sectionals" with each musical family in your band or orchestra. Many times, you can talk to your pool of private teachers and get help with those group coaching sessions.

Continuing YOUR Education is Important

It's also important for you as a band or orchestra director to continue your study on instruments you don't know. One year, study the violin, next year, study the trumpet or trombone, the next year, clarinet, or something else. The more you know about each instrument, the better you become as a music teacher. If you have time after all that, please continue to practice on your own major instrument to improve your insight and growth.

The early stages of learning are the most important for creating good habits. I don't know about you, but in my college years (50+ years ago) we got one semester of study on each family of instruments. That is simply not enough study to successfully start a student on an instrument in the early stages.

INTRODUCING MUSICAL INSTRUMENTS

Let's start at the beginning. A young student either hears one of your more advanced ensembles that comes to their school and/or the elementary school music teacher takes over and helps the student select an instrument they may be interested in.

The next step is for the student and their parents to rent or purchase an instrument *that works*.

A tall order.

Where I live, there is a store that specializes in woodwind instruments and services for beginning to more advanced students, and even for professionals who are encouraged to hang out to enhance the atmosphere of the store. They also have a repair shop that specializes in woodwinds. You may or may not be so lucky.

This music store will see that students get a rental instrument that's in proper repair and of good enough quality to play easily.

In addition, my local store will make sure that there is a good mouthpiece, reed, and ligature in the case. These are *the* key ingredients to getting a sound on an instrument, along with some luck. Without these ingredients, there is very little chance of success.

There are also good new and used instruments available for

purchase from a bona fide woodwind dealer who can advise you on price vs. quality and resale value. This is always one of the most important initial decisions—to rent or buy.

Also, keep in mind the physical size of a beginning student. Alto sax is almost always the choice, as a tenor sax is just too big for most youngsters. The same is true for all members of the woodwind family.

If your local music store is run by a trumpet player, a string player, a percussionist, or anything except a woodwind player they are renting or selling to you on hearsay or just using salesmanship. This is something you will want to know about them.

I have two videos on YouTube entitled "Starting Music" and "A First Clarinet" that discuss whether to rent or buy an instrument. You will want to make sure to take a moment to consider what I have to say there. Now is a good time for that.

Clarinet, Saxophone and Flute

Can we agree that it's important to have a good instrument, a good mouthpiece, and a good reed and ligature? For the flute, of course, the headjoint is the mouthpiece and can make it easier or more difficult for the flute to be played (*especially the second octave and the low notes*).

Oboe and Bassoon

The oboe and bassoon require a great reed, as that is the mouthpiece and sound-producing mechanism. For oboe and bassoon, even your local music store might not understand where to get good reeds of the correct hardness and quality. I believe these instruments require a private teacher from the beginning.

Ok, so now we have a good instrument for our youngsters, and they come to their first school rehearsal. I need not tell you the difficulties ahead of you. This is where your practice time on one instrument every year can be a big advantage to you. You are now standing in front of most likely 10 to 40 young, somewhat empty minds that are, in theory, more confused than you are.

SQUARE ONE

It's imperative that you teach the students how to properly assemble and hold the instrument, so they are not breaking mouthpieces, reeds, or other parts while taking the instrument out of the case or putting it back in. It sounds easy. However, small children are not always that coordinated, nor do they have a routine for getting instruments in and out of a case, so it's easy to drop the horn.

THE FIRST LESSON

My suggestion is that, though you may have a method book, you should plan to dedicate the first group lesson to learning one common note *(I will only talk about woodwinds from here on)*. Along with this one note, the student needs to know how to practice. And on the first lesson, learning how to practice means playing one note with the appropriate amount of air. If you can impart these ideas while teaching how to assemble the instrument in the first hour, you have accomplished a lot.

FOR THE PARENTS

Of course, there are always parents who want their child to study an instrument just to introduce them to music *(oh please don't make my child a musician!)*. They treat it like karate, swimming, or any other extracurricular pursuit. I have no suggestion for you here. However, I am sure that if you are experienced, you have learned how to deal with this situation.

You can remind parents to encourage at least an introduction to music for their child. For the young student, music, as with many artistic subjects, can provide one of the most important and necessary skills: Having a more complete education and being a well-rounded student, with the ability to listen and appreciate the international language of music. Encourage private lessons and ask the parent to sit through most private lessons so they can help the student at home as if it was math or English.

It's important to convey information to the parents as to how the student will be expected to practice, and that in the beginning, a few minutes a couple of times a day might be fine, but as the year(s) go by, more commitment is necessary. I have found that much of my lesson time is spent just reminding students—from beginning to advanced—*how* to practice. You may even suggest having some woodwind music playing around the house. Concept is everything at this point.

It's also important to get an address, email, telephone, and any other information so you can keep the parents informed. They need to know what you expect the student to practice. Be sure to tell the parents and students where and when there are concerts or clinics that the students should attend. And provide your information so the parents can be encouraged to talk to you.

Parents need to know that woodwind study requires knowledge of breath control and muscle building. They also need to know that the student must become acclimated to the sound of their instrument. Encourage parents to buy recordings, both solo and in ensembles of all styles. They can just play them and not require the student to listen. If the music is playing, they will listen. Your suggestions of recording repertoire, as a teacher, may be appreciated.

PRACTICE AND LISTENING SCHEDULE

My feeling is that it is more important for the student to practice *some* amount every day than how long they practice. Especially in the beginning, it's the habit of taking the instrument out of the case, putting it together, and blowing a note that's important. So, a minimum practice is one minute a day. If they can't manage that, perhaps music is not for them.

It's important to remind the student they are holding a foreign object, and that they need to learn to hold the instrument until they are comfortable just holding the horn in a relaxed manner, both in the playing position and at rest. They can hold the instrument while watching television just to acclimate.

Remember that all wind instruments require the student to learn how to use air (how to breathe, how to blow, and how to coordinate that with the embouchure and tongue, which are muscles that need to be slowly developed).

Much like a child who never reads is not likely to become an English major or author, a music student who does not listen to music will have a difficult time developing a concept of sound or "a good ear." The student must know how they are expected to sound and how to develop that sound. You might suggest band or orchestra recordings that you know your young musicians will appreciate.

Sometimes parents are so overwhelmed with life they don't want to sit through the lesson. They are happy just to get a half hour alone away from their lovely little child. This will really slow down the learning curve. The student must know the parent is interested and encouraging.

So, let's call this the end of part one.

What to Teach a Beginning Woodwind Student

"FOR SCHOOL TEACHERS"
Part 2

Usually I put these ezines out every couple of months or so; however with school starting soon, I thought it might be good to offer you the teacher, and the parent a few more ideas.

Teacher Dilemma

Unless you can play the student's instrument and mouthpiece/headjoint/reed set-up in some sort of sanitary way, you cannot know what the student is feeling. The feeling is much of the tactile method of success of any instrument. And many student instruments are not in playing condition.

Student Expectations

You have had your first week with the new students and this is your second meeting with them. It's important for you to let them know that they will be tested on a regular basis in front of the other students on the assignment from the previous week. Peer acknowledgment becomes very important with this type of expected learning compliance. Teachers can teach, parents can monitor, but in my experience, only peers in the beginning are an influence in having any student come in prepared.

Students just don't want to be embarrassed.

The first week, you gave each student a note to learn. Go from student to student and ask them to play the first note they learned and say the name of the note. If you have decided to use a band method, have them play the first line. This is a good time to check some important basic elements.

Add a Second Note

After you have gone through the group with each student playing, introduce a second note of the chromatic scale. Again, let the students know you expect them to be able to play the note, recite the name of the note, and show you on a piece of music where the note is. (It may be time for you to make sure each student has a manuscript book). You are closer to giving the students an octave of *the alphabet of music,* **the chromatic scale.** The faster the students learn this scale, the more they will be able to concentrate on counting. It only takes 12 weeks to learn one octave of the chromatic scale, adding one note per week. It's well worth the time—in addition to any band method you are using.

As each student plays:

For clarinet and sax: Make sure their reed is on the mouthpiece correctly and that the reed does not look like it has been chewed on. **Remind them that they need at least 5 reeds in their case ready to play.** They should be playing on a 1.5 or 2 reed at this point unless they have a very open or closed mouthpiece. They need to build face muscles (embouchure) gradually.

Having a fairly new reed well placed on a fairly good mouthpiece will save you, the teacher, an immense amount of time.

Notice how much mouthpiece they take and what their embouchure is trying to do to create a tone. **The most important thing you can do in this process is to get the students to play the same volume.** There will be a lot of variance in how much each student thinks they need to blow and how much mouthpiece they need to take. *Remember that the more mouthpiece they take the harder the reed becomes.* Keep reminding them to blow the air towards the bell of the instrument. Urge the ones that are holding back to blow harder and the ones that are blasting to control the sound *a little.*

It's a lot easier in the long run to fix a student's sound that blows too loud, as opposed to those children who are holding back.

This is also a good time to remind the students to sit up with their heads in a normal position facing forward. If a student is looking down, raise the music stand so they must look up to see the note.

For the flute: I want to explain to you how the sound and octaves are actually produced. There are many misconceptions about creating a flute sound.

Think of a circular target (like an archery target) on the wall. If we hold a water hose and point it at the target and turn on the hose enough that the water hits the center of the target, we can consider this the basic correct sound (but not technique; more on that soon). If we lower the water pressure, the stream goes below the center of the target (*pitch goes flat*) and if we raise the pressure the water goes above the target (*sharp*).

If we keep the pressure the same and walk closer to the target, we get more splash back (or rolled in at the blow hole), and if we walk farther away from the target the stream goes below the target (which means the only chance of getting the second octave is to blow much harder). *Though farther down the teaching line it is important to remember the way to get the 2nd octave is to get the air pressure closer to the target with the lips coming forward.* Rolling the flute in will give us the second octave by bringing the lips closer to the back wall of the blow hole and will give us a flat sound and lack of volume that is not desirable. Blowing harder will also create the 2nd octave, as it's the same as getting the lips closer to the back of the blow hole but will likely be sharp.

Another variable to sound on the flute is the size of the air stream. Some students will have a very big embouchure hole (less air pressure) and some a smaller one (more pressure). The smaller one is desired.

Make sure the jaw is open and loose so the student is not blowing through their teeth.

The target/water stream is a description of how the air works. Despite the hypothetical ideas I gave above on how the air (water) stream works, it's important to know that the correct concept for the flute sound in the beginning is to have about half of the blow hole covered and blow down much like a glass pop bottle. The flute is held with the chin, the middle of the first finger of the left hand on the body of the flute, the right thumb of the underbody of the flute, with the little finger on the Eb key on the far end of the flute. This should create the correct balance points.

The flute should be put together so when looking down the keywork from the top, that the center of the blow hole is aligned with the center of the keys on the flute and the foot joint is aligned with the keys a little to the outside (or away) from the center of the main key section.

As an exception to all other woodwinds that go in the mouth, the flute must be balanced and the finger position (as on all instruments really) is of utmost importance. In general, the flute should be parallel to the floor and turned left over the left leg at a 90-degree angle with the body. This frees up the tension in the upper body.

A good thing for a flute player to do is to take the headjoint off and blow directly into the blowhole, rocking it back and forth until the most comfortable sound comes out. Then they should hold a sound, with the good feeling of a "sweet spot" on the headjoint. Now add the headjoint to the flute and they will notice it's easier to get a sound.

Now the oboe and bassoon! If you absolutely cannot get the parents to provide a private teacher, make sure the student is starting with a soft reed. Learning the fingering is the same as any instrument, however the embouchure development is much like weightlifting. It's important that the student be putting minimum pressure on the reed to get a sound. Students should practice for a minute or two at a time at first, and gradually increase in time and the strength of the reed over many years. If air is coming out of the side of the mouth, there is an embouchure problem or the student is fatigued. In the beginning, fatigue comes quickly.

Tonguing and stopping the air for sax, clarinet, oboe, and bassoon: The tongue should start the air by thinking the syllable "TU" and touching the tip of the tongue to an area just under the tip of the reed. The farther down the reed, the harsher the tonguing sounds. This is because more cane must be moved to get the sound. The tongue should not attack the reed, but rather approach the reed as if they were going to touch a hot plate with the tongue. This encourages the tongue to retreat quickly. Under no circumstances should the tongue be used *between* the mouthpiece and the reed. To stop the air, simply stop blowing without letting the embouchure loosen. When the tongue is not in use it should be lying motionless and relaxed in the bottom of the mouth.

Tonguing on the flute: The flutist should simply silently imitate the syllable "TU" in the normal place they would say it. Many flutists tongue in the front of their mouth, between the teeth, and you will be able to see the tongue trying to start the tone there. This is to be discouraged. Stopping the tone is done simply by stopping blowing or taking a breath without letting the embouchure loosen at the same time. When the tongue is not in use, it should be lying motionless and relaxed at the bottom of the mouth.

In the case of all woodwinds, a tongue that is raised anywhere while playing a long note indicates that the support is too high, most likely in the solar plexus or the neck and throat.

Practice Habits: I've always been an afternoon and evening person, so I generally practice between 3 and 7 PM in the late afternoon. Other people are morning people and get up at 5:30 AM ready to get at it. What I am suggesting here is that based on the students' very busy schedules and body clocks, that practice takes place at the same approximate time and place every day. Again, it's not as much about how much time they practice, especially in the beginning, but how regular the practice is. It's *the habit* of practice that must be cultivated. Students should split their practice time between the material that a private instructor gives them and what the band director expects from them. Most usually the students who study privately will be far ahead of the regular music class and may only require a refresher day to come in prepared compared to the average level of students.

Learning to read music: In the beginning, there are hurdles to be overcome to enable the student to actually look at the music. There is a lot going on in your room and the kids are paying attention to anything and everything. This makes it hard for them to look at a note or anything on a page. The student may also be an "ear" player (which is very good) but needs to be constantly reminded to watch the notes and rhythms. Or, it just may not occur to them to look at music on a music stand, as opposed to being at a school desk.

This is another reason to emphasize the learning of an octave or octave and a half of the chromatic scale (the alphabet of music) over several weeks. If the student can play and recite the name of the notes in the chromatic scale it takes the hurdle of note recognition away and they can concentrate on rhythm.

The combination of ear training and eye training at a young age is something most of us did not get. It was either one or the other. This is a big gift to a musician, especially at a young age.

Mouthpiece set-up: I had planned to talk about the subject in this ezine, however after consideration, it is almost a book. You can go to my YouTube and put "Mike Vaccaro" in the search box and several of my instructional videos about mouthpieces, reeds, and ligatures can be found there. (By the way, there is also a sports writer of the same name.) If you have a music store near you that specializes in woodwinds or has a specialist for woodwinds, ask that person to look at your instrument and mouthpiece set-up and advise you. This is just too big of a subject to generalize about, though ultimately, it is one of the most important.

The idea of the instrument and all the extra things that go with it, like reeds and ligatures are the things that can make music fun or a nightmare. Just think, if someone handed your student a perfect playing setup that they had to change very little over the years, what an advantage they would have. For your sake, I want it to be *easy*. Parents, invested in their child's music education should be cultivated and this subject should be discussed freely in your communications with them.

I hope this helps you in the initial stages of teaching woodwind instrumentalists. It's come to my attention that many beginners start on the recorder before they proceed to a band or orchestra instruments and its problems. A good idea for sure.

> *Working hard for something we*
> *don't care about is called stress.*
> *Working hard for something we love*
> *is called passion.*
> —**Simon Sinek**

Educators and Administrators Alert!

First, let me say that these K-12 teachers, and the college students aspiring to enter music pedagogy, are the angels of the whole musical scene.

One of the subjects I touched on was the state of music education for K-12 teachers, and the travesty presented to them in instrument classes. That's where you study a family of instruments for 16 weeks and then go on to another family of instruments for the next 16 weeks. Woodwinds, brass, percussion, and strings in just 64 weeks over 2 years.

No one can convince me that they can even learn the basics of clarinet, sax, flute, oboe, and bassoon in 16 weeks. As I said in my lecture, these students, training to be teachers, are about one page in front of their own potential students when they start. By the time a teacher, trained in this manner, has spent a few months on the job, these same teachers are at least a page behind the student.

If this is the scenario we're dealing with, it's important for all students to study privately to develop in a timely manner. To add to the dilemma, this is one of the more time-consuming disciplines, and most band programs at the elementary and junior high only have one hour a week with the students.

Not only is it 64 weeks to learn every instrument in the orchestra and be able to teach them, but they must do it while thinking of junior and senior recitals, private lessons, and practicing on their major instrument, marching band, and re-studying the basics of history, philosophy and math, etc. for the umpteenth time. Some students are even studying the Business of Music at the few places it's taught.

Let's face it, not all music students are going to be teachers or professionals. That makes Music Business classes mandatory. ADMINISTRATORS, please accept and fix this situation!!!

Back to the K-12 group *and their administrators:* Are the administrators even aware that this isn't enough study time on each instrument, much less each family of instruments? I challenge administrators to find a new way to give their college students more time to get to know their subject matter. How about a whole year for each family of instruments?

I don't claim to know the problems of music administrators, but I have seen the problems of the teachers who graduate and don't know how a middle G on the trumpet feels, or who can't read viola clef and play a C, G, Bb, or Eb scale on the viola. I asked the room how many people knew how to create an octave on the flute and out of a group of 40 educators only 2 people raised their hands. This is a perfect example of what I am talking about.

The only suggestion I could give the educators at the seminar was to study an instrument privately from an outstanding teacher and then, after the first year, switch to another instrument. By the time they near the end of their career, they just *might* have a pretty good idea of what a student feels on several instruments. The dilemma is that the teachers, in many cases, have started a family, might be practicing their principal instrument, working long hours and have the vicissitudes of adult life to deal with—tough to get a half-hour or hour on a new instrument, as a beginner and still get ample rest to deal with the students. But as I always say, start off with a minute a day.

I leave it to the administrators along with the university or college to do *something* for our music teachers and their students *as soon as you can* because **the system must change!!!**

Zen and Jazz

When the great Jazz critic Nate Hentoff was asked, "What is Jazz?" Nate, replied, "If you have to ask, I can't tell you!"

The same could be said of any form of music: Classical, Pop, Country Western, Klezmer, Middle Eastern, Chinese, Japanese, etc.

> *"In Zen there is an understanding that goes, 'Only speak poetry to a poet!' This does not mean that you have to be a musician to experience jazz, but rather, a certain understanding or mindset that when a listener hears it, they need no explanation of what it is or what they are experiencing. They get it!"*

To me, this is "facing the music." In other words, being able to listen to music without a preconceived notion or prejudice; to be able to *hear* the music, despite what you are used to listening to; to be able to see the truth in what you don't know. "To get it." That doesn't mean to like it necessarily, but to hear the essence of it.

> *"It's just like the story in birth of Zen, when the Buddha held up a flower, to see if anyone of his disciples understood this gesture, only one monk, seeing this immediately, understood—Zen was born. A mind-to-mind realization of understanding that needs no explanation took place."*

"For those trying to get an intellectual definition of either Zen or Jazz, it's like trying to draw a line in the water with your finger! It's the black hole of language! To say what Zen is, is to show one's ignorance. It's like grasping at air! Art transcends language!"

"In Jazz improvisation, it's where the musician is both the creator and the created. It transcends reason! It unfolds from nowhere! It's an ever blossoming of an idea and yet it does not appear until it happens! The player is just as surprised and turned on by what is unfolding, as is the listener! Like Zen, there is no subject and object! There is no separation between the doer and the doing!"

"There just is! As D.T. Suzuki states so well in, "Essays in Zen," Therefore the finite is the infinite and vice versa. These are not two separate things, though we are compelled to conceive them so intellectually." The past, future, and present evaporate moment to moment, as both the artist and the art evolves transcending itself."

"Some questions just cannot be answered, nor should they be! This is not a condescending remark, but to say that there are no words to adequately describe "what is Jazz," and if one has to be told, then no amount of words will do."

Make no mistake though, Jazz is improvisation on musical theory that has been studied and learned.

The same is true for any music. When the musician is no longer thinking about how to play something because they know the subject matter so well, it comes from the heart, or the spirit, or the cosmos, whether improvised or not. That is the moment of freedom for the performer, which makes it so much easier for the listener to be charmed by the music.

In this modern world, due to budgets and time and travel restraints, it becomes harder and harder to get enough rehearsal time to know the music without thinking—to own it by reacting. It seems we are all in such a hurry to do all the things required in modern life, that we have less time to bathe in the music. The artists who do that seldom get rewarded financially and understand why.

True freedom is reached not by playing or improvising the music, or reading it on the page, but by owning it to the point of being at one with the notes and the music.

With Jazz, there is always the improvisation. But even in free improvisation, not based on a chord structure, the music must always be from the foundation of mastery, to let the music be the centerpiece—not the performance, the performer, or the audience.

It's like what is said about grabbing for air. We can't grab at it, which is foolish, but if we are aware, we can be with it.

We have all had the experience of being at one with something. The idea is to practice that feeling and the mental peace of that moment. Babies have it. But as we learn to talk or play music, or paint, dance or act, we must work on being one with life, as is the baby—or that moment we have all had, when we were at one with something. When we were there, but not involved intellectually.

Under pressure, you don't rise to the occasion,
you sink to the level of your training.
—Anonymous Navy Seal
From the Noa Kageyama Blog

Recovering from the Bumps in Your Musical Journey

From time to time, we all must jump over, or at least avoid, small and large hurdles in our lives. *Life's hurdles* are those things that we must jump over, go around, or plow through to maintain our life rhythm. We all must jump over, or at least try to avoid these hurdles in our lives. These hurdles also affect our musical life. They simply get in the way of our plans.

Here are some big hurdles that are obvious: injury to yourself or a family member, sickness, hospitalization, births, deaths, major auto accidents, divorce, marriage, and other big items. You can add your own big hurdles to this list. These are events that make you stop what you are doing and be in the life moment.

Then there are the minor hurdles, which are many—just everyday inconveniences that slow us down. They could include an argument with a spouse or workmate, a flat tire or some other auto-related minor incident, slow service in a restaurant or other place of business that makes you late, looking for your keys or glasses, minor depression, laziness, a minor problem with your instrument, terrible traffic, and the list goes on and on—every single day.

How do we cope?

The smallest hurdles can be ignored while our practice routines continue, whereas navigating the larger hurdles may take some time, attention, and effort before returning to our normal routines.

After a major hurdle, if we are still inclined to play music, we have to build back our "chops" (i.e. embouchure, bowing technique, the ability to see and hear the music, or whatever your particular instrument or voice requires.)

The first thing to do, to get back in performance shape, is to *start practicing on a regular basis.*

If we are upset or depressed, practicing will make us feel better, since the act of playing music puts our attention outside of ourselves. This helps us take our minds off of our dilemmas.

It's time to gain our strength back, coordinate our fingers with what we see on the page or in our minds, and learn to listen with 100% commitment again. Please take your time and be patient. It takes some time to overcome a major hurdle. You will do it, I am sure.

Start slow, be easy on yourself, take plenty of breaks, start with a few minutes, and increase your time daily.

As your physical and/or mental strength improves, your practicing will tend to improve at the same rate. Revisit some pieces in your repertoire, look at some new music that you have been thinking about approaching, and just try and settle into a routine that may or may not have eluded you.

The important thing is that you try to miss as few days as possible while re-establishing the practice habit, to the point where you meet your normal practice commitment or even increase it. As usual, it's best if we can maintain our normal practice start times, or if needed to accommodate a lifestyle change, set a time that is repeatable daily.

I have often contended that it's not how much time we practice, but that we do it on a regular basis with a commitment to concentration.

It's easy to be charmed by music (or by the puzzle of music), which creates the desire to spend *more* time rather than *less* time practicing.

When you encounter a hurdle, make sure you recognize it. Recognizing the big hurdles is easy while becoming aware of the little hurdles can be more vexing to find and correct.

Pay attention to your hurdles.

#24

RETIREMENT
(How to Do It)

While it hasn't always been that way, my number one mantra to my students, my friends, or to you in these little musings is:

SAVE YOUR MONEY.

Why is that important? Simply stated, it's because if you are lucky, you will retire, and if you treated yourself well, you may even retire active and healthy. Either way, you *will* need money to enter the last couple of semesters of your life.

Do you have an idea about when you want to retire and how you want to live your life after your years of work? If so, the time to launch your plan is the day you start your first job. You may even have some money from childhood savings or odd jobs.

I was not very good at saving until I turned 50 and suddenly realized that I was going to retire at some point if I stayed alive (*assume that you are going to stay alive*). Along with a small inheritance, the Musicians Pension Fund, and savings (after 50), I was able to retire comfortably. Oh, and there was also the Musicians Special Payments Fund for residuals that helps.

I was lucky. I was always a union guy. I know that's geeky nowadays, but what it did though was save money *for* me, without my having to think about retirement.

It's not quite that way anymore. Unions are on a downward slide. Employers want more money as they have become greedy. There are too many talented people in almost every field, so employers can hire people for less because of competition. And then there is technology, which eats a lot of jobs as well. So now each of us . . . *well you* . . . must take care of yourself.

I hope that each of you can find a bunch of free money for retirement. But if you don't have that, it's time to be serious about saving, perhaps investing, or perhaps judiciously buying a property that will appreciate. I think you know what I am saying. *Don't wait until you are 50 years old like I did.*

Even if your family has money, and you expect to receive some or all of it sometime in your life, it is still important to save money. Why? If you believe "we are what we do on a daily basis," then the art of saving will make us rich or at least relatively rich. That is, rich enough to make at least what we were making when we were working.

The piggy bank we all had as children was a good lesson in saving, for the few of us who paid attention to it.

With the influx of a younger and more educated workforce, there is increased competition. Not only that, but also there are also personality clashes that come with any type of job. These must be approached with a smile and a willingness to compromise when one is able to.

We must realize that ALL jobs are political, even in music.

In music, as in any occupation, there are parts of the job that are less fun than others. Those parts of the job can become tedious, but we must persevere to get to the parts we love.

The future comes sooner than we think. Why? Because we are busy and energetic. We can keep up with the pace of modern life and work

16 hours a day, have a family, and have a lot of fun too. As we age, like an old car, the parts of the body start talking to us, and our youthful injuries revisit us. It's more difficult to keep up with the pace of life. The world is moving faster than we want it to. A retirement plan allows us to slow down our pace naturally, at a time of our own choosing, and look more closely at what is important.

Not only in the music arena, but in many disciplines, including accounting, schools simply don't teach about money management, career development, or saving methods for retirement. Young people are left alone to figure it out, or if they are from a wealthy family, study firsthand how it's done. Saving or attaining wealth for a comfortable retirement is something that must be monitored on a regular basis. It's as important as practicing for musicians.

This may mean giving up unnecessary "treats" while paying oneself first to ensure a continually growing nest egg. We live in a world of excesses in the United States, with advertisers badgering us from every angle. This can be avoided if we live simply. How many of us have a garage full of things we bought that we will rarely, if ever, use—skeletons of our past, and/or current buying habits? Speaking of unnecessary treats, using drugs and alcohol in excess slows us down and takes important money from our future. It freezes us where we are when the habit becomes in full bloom.

My music teacher, a professional freelance musician, always used to tell me: "Pay yourself first." It makes sense to pay yourself before you pay your bills. Take a percentage of your earnings *(10% sounds good)* and put that amount away *every* time you make money. By cash or check. You will be amazed how quickly you find your nest egg increasing.

The banks and credit card companies don't care how much you pay on your debt because that's how they make their money. If we think of the credit card, and credit in general, as a convenience card, pay it off monthly and generally keep a zero balance, all the interest we would have paid is savings we can use to pay ourselves with. We don't have to skimp. We just must not waste. Seems like a pretty good plan for retirement.

Another young lady, advanced for her age, told me, "keep your overhead low." This is another way of having money to save. Along with *pay yourself first*, this is the best information I ever received. This is truly the art of saving. Another good plan? I think so.

In music, and many other fields, most of us are independent contractors, so it makes sense to keep our overhead low. Many of our employers and much of the government hope that we all would be independent contractors, as it makes their life easier.

If we are musicians, we have big investments to make in instruments, the tools of our craft. If we *have* to use credit, it's better to use a commercial credit institution than a credit card. *Use credit wisely.*

One thing we haven't discussed so far is health. If you can take care of your body by not participating in radical sports, and if you can eat in a healthy manner, and stay away from abusing alcohol and drugs, those are other ways to save money. As you well know, medical care is very expensive these days.

So now what?

That is simply why all the talk of overhead, health, and savings is about—Retirement.

We are retired. We are most likely as busy as we have ever been. But we have the opportunity of doing what we want. We may even retire early while the body is still near its zenith.

That doesn't necessarily mean that we will stop working or stop being involved in anything important to us. It means we won't *have* to do the things at our job(s) that we really didn't like to do.

The angst of *having* to make a living will be over.

You have the choice of becoming, or remaining, an active participant in *life*.

OR, you can sit and watch TV all day. Either way, the choice is yours, and you'll have enough money to support your choice.

There is a difference in giving up and
knowing when you have had enough.
—Unknown

Remember you must **write your plan down**, so you don't circle-think it in your head and never see what you are doing. The plan can change but please *write it down*. Also, if you decide that 10% is the amount you are going to save, keep a ledger. See it every time you make it. There was a very busy Italian musician and he worked 16-hour days for at least 60 years. The joke was every time it rained his pool turned green. That was the old Italian way. No banks, no investments. Just put the money in a tin can and bury it. Probably not the best plan but a plan that works and guarantees a good retirement.

That is simply why all the talk of overhead,
health, and savings is about—*Retirement.*

No one may succeed in life without saving money.
There is no exception to this rule,
and no one may escape it.
—Napoleon Hill

To do much clear thinking,
a person must arrange
for regular periods of solitude,
when he can concentrate and indulge
his imagination without distraction.
—Thomas A. Edison

An aim in life is the only fortune worth finding;
and it is not to be found in foreign lands,
but in the heart itself.
—Robert Louis Stevenson

If you cannot do great things yourself,
remember that you can do small things in a great way.
—Napoleon Hill

The best compensation for doing things
is the ability to do more.
—Napoleon Hil

Off the Beaten Path

This is the first, and most likely the last time that I will present an ezine about myself. It's an excerpt from an interview with me conducted by Bill Payne*.

You can also find a video on (**www.performingartsreview.net**), Daniel Kepl's site. This is, of course, in addition to the "Introduction" at the beginning of this book.

Many of you have been reading these broadcasts and don't know who I am or what I have done in the music business. Since these "musings" are always about the music "business" and the difficulties that surround the actual playing of music, I thought that some information about myself might be helpful.

To those of you who do know me, you may find out something you didn't know (or care to know}, but I hope you will at least find the following interview interesting.

My next broadcast will be back to the business of music and the life of music makers.

*https://www.linkedin.com/pulse/bill-payne-pens-interview-me-mike-vaccaro/?trk=portfolio_article-card_title

A Woodwind Player for All Seasons —
Mike Vaccaro!

Woodwind player Mike Vaccaro has had a career in the music business that many musicians just dream about. This interview will touch on a few highlights. His 50-year pursuit has taken him on an adventure that has included most styles of classical, jazz, and popular music. Above and beyond his music career, he has made improvements to the design of the clarinet. He also makes custom-made clarinet, bass clarinet, and sax mouthpieces.

1. What was your young life like growing up in California? Are there any other musicians or artists in your extended family?

I grew up in rural Los Angeles. Even though it was only 15 minutes from downtown, it was called Rivera when I moved there in about 1953, and it annexed with the neighboring city to become Pico Rivera in the 60s sometime.

When I moved there it was 3 rows of houses in miles and miles of orange groves. The 5 Freeway didn't go past our house yet, and it was finally completed to Harbor Boulevard when Disneyland opened. Until then, the major highway was Telegraph Road. Despite this rural beginning, the orange trees were quickly cut down over just a few years (ruining our playpen) and what was rural became the suburbs.

The public school system was good, and our band director, who visited once a week was outstanding. Leon Guide was patient and understood his job and was a professional musician playing casuals on the weekend. In junior high he saw us daily.

High school was another good experience with Robert Strecker, a professional musician who we scared away his first year of teaching. Then John Jacobs, who had a long career teaching in high school and junior college took over. Through most of that time I studied privately with Stan Seckler, who played with the Long Beach Civic Light Opera, and taught a lot of half hour private lessons at Pico Music.

2. What attracted you to the idea of becoming a woodwind player? What horn did you start on, and who were the artists that caught your ear first?

I took up the clarinet when I was in the 4th grade when we all started music in the district. My parents bought me recordings of Benny Goodman and Sol Yaged when I rented the clarinet. Then tenor sax was added in the 8th grade. As a senior in high school, I added the flute. By the time I left college to go on the road, I was messing with the oboe, but not seriously. It was not a conscious thought to add the instruments; I just was always interested in learning something new. In about 9th grade I heard Count Basie's band at Disneyland and sitting in the front row I decided that's what I wanted to do for a living. I wanted to be a professional musician. It was a very early age to know what I wanted to do.

3. Were you interested in any music specifically (pop, jazz, classical) or did the enjoyment of all music pique your eagerness?

I really knew nothing about the enormity of music. During my formative years, I was interested in everything I heard. At the time, my only playing interests were concert band and stage band, as those were my only opportunities to perform. My home life was mainly limited to Perry Como recordings and the like played on a 78-rpm record player. Cerritos Junior College was a great place to hear music and be associated with professional musicians. The Collegiate Neophonic, co-sponsored by Stan Kenton and Conn Instruments, put the best musicians from all the local colleges together. At Cal State Long Beach, I played in the band and orchestra. About 16 of us started a clandestine jazz band, which eventually became the beginnings of one of the first commercial music programs in the country, despite the disgust of many of the old-time professors.

4. Early gigs . . . Did you have your own band or did you work for other leaders?

Larry Walters, my trumpet-playing friend and I had a band in elementary school. We played the theme from *Zorro*, got a dollar apiece, and a free dinner for the PTA meeting. In high school I played in the Silvertones, a band led by Terry Purrington, and we won the battle of the bands at the Hollywood Bowl. I also played in the Pico Rivera Stage Band headed by my private teacher, Stan Seckler. At CSULB I played in the clandestine stage band previously mentioned, and also with a small group that Richard and Karen Carpenter put together that went around to various schools and performed the *Marquis de Sade*, a popular record album at the time.

At CSULB I also performed the *Scaramouche* by Darius Milhaud, for Alto Sax and Orchestra, which was the West Coast premiere, with the composer present. The concert was sponsored by the French embassy and I was honored to be selected as the soloist by Henri Temianka, the school Orchestra director and world-famous string quartet performer. It was fabulous playing for a professional musician, as his approach was different than the other teachers. We also learned a lot over a beer at the local bar. He was a man of distinction, with many memories of the business.

5. When was the decision made that you were going to concentrate on becoming a doubler? How did that come about? Was it just an evolving necessity from what leaders needed from you or was it the plan from the beginning once you saw yourself as a complete working professional?

I was just always into learning more and studying woodwinds seemed the way to do it. I played with the Collegiate Neophonic which required all kinds of doubles. It was partially funded by Stan Kenton, with Jack Wheaton and Don Erjavec running the semi-weekly rehearsals. It was a good contact as Bill Fritz coached us, and when he quit the Kenton Band, he recommended me. So off on the road I went in my junior year of college with a mostly classical background, never to go back to formal schooling.

6. Who were your teachers? What advice did you receive from your mentors that still holds true even now . . .

The early teachers I have already discussed, but in college I hooked up with Ralph Gari. My father had just died after I graduated from high school and Ralph became not only my mentor, but a substitute father figure as well. He was to help greatly later on in my career. We had a wonderful sax quartet 20 years after I studied with him, and did an LP entitled *Saxes 4*. I think that it can still be found in rare record shops on the Internet.

The best teacher for teaching me music (not technique) was Luella Howard. She was first flute in the Los Angeles Philharmonic for many years, becoming first flute at 20th Century Fox for the remainder of her career. She taught me phrasing—the most important thing we can learn.

Looking back to my elementary school teacher, Leon Guide, I remember standing next to his car one day and asking him what I should do if I became a musician. He said, "Be good at a lot of things." I think this helped guide me in my musical and business interests (I started to listen to all types of music). I always had a little music-related side business. I even quit playing for 8 years to become a full-fledged production company working with large corporations at their yearly meetings with entertainment and all that goes with it.

When I went back to playing full time, that business turned into a music contracting business, and I've been the Music Contractor at the Cerritos Center for the Performing Arts since it opened 30 years ago. I have also contracted live and recorded music of all types.

7. I know that you were on the road with Woody Herman and Stan Kenton. How did you get those gigs? Talk for a second about playing bass saxophone with Stan Kenton.

As I previously indicated, Bill Fritz got me the Kenton job. I had to borrow a baritone saxophone from the Conn Company that Stan arranged for, as I didn't own the instrument. As the Conn rep said, "You are the Conn artist and I am the Conn man." The bass sax was provided by the band. By the time I got on the Kenton Band, the bass sax was only being used on four or five arrangements, and after about three months I talked Stan out of using it. It was transposable on the baritone anyway. Don Rader, another coach with the Neophonic, recommended me to Woody's band. During that period, I also played in the Paul Horn Flute Ensemble (four flutes and rhythm section) sponsored by the Conn Music Company.

8. In the world of big band music, Stan Kenton was a striking presence. How was he as a person? I understand that he traveled with the band on the infamous band bus. Is there an amusing story that you could relate to us that happened on the road?

Stan was the Great White Father, and for me, another father substitute. I was on the band during the period of the Dee Barton recording *Stan Kenton Conducts the Music of Dee Barton*. A great band and great arrangements. I also did a tour of military bases that was not much fun at all despite the good arrangements of standards.

The camaraderie on the various Kenton band busses was always great. You must understand that in those times there were no specialized touring busses as there are now. We were basically in a Greyhound bus, sometimes for 12 to 16 hours a day, and even worse, sometimes for 6 or 7 days in a row. There was always a band member vendor who would buy lots of beer and keep it cold, and when we ran out of booze, he would overcharge us to get beer. Smart marketing for musicians who weren't thinking that far ahead.

Stan *always* wore a suit. After a long overnight ride, when we rolled up to a hotel, he would comb his hair, and be the first one out of the bus to help get the luggage out of the bins. There is a **Stan Kenton Appreciation Group** on Facebook that I urge fans to sign up on. Many stories are chronicled there.

9. How did you end up in Las Vegas?

We did a two-week stint with the Woody Herman Band, and Ralph Gari, my college teacher, was working up there again (he spent most of his career there). I would hang out with him and when a chair opened up at the Follies at the Tropicana, I took over the position. It was a great opportunity (despite playing the same music two times a night for a year). Ralph got me in the Las Vegas Symphony and Las Vegas Chamber Players, as well. I regularly played in a "kix" band at the union until 5 AM several nights a week. I left Vegas for a year and then came back for two years at the Sands, playing with some great celebrities and singers. Again I joined the symphony and chamber players. What happens in Vegas stays in Vegas, and yes it was wild and crazy!

10. Please talk about your chamber trio MUSIQUE, one of my favorite groups. Your playing on "Caprice for C Clarinet" was over the top. How did you meet the composer Jack Reidling and the singer Judith Dunlore?

When I finally left Las Vegas for good, Judith Dunlore, my wife and I went to Germany. I had a job offer and she wanted to take opera auditions. With no planning, ahead we went, and it turns out it was the wrong season for opera auditions, and I didn't like the band I was with—and they really didn't like me. So, after four months of traveling around Europe we came back and landed in Long Beach, California. It took me a couple of years to regain my musical contacts and in the meantime, we met Jack Reidling at the union building. He wanted to play the woodwind and vocal literature and we were delighted to find a musical partner. We practiced 6 hours a day 3 days a week for a year before putting on our first concert and doing our first recording. Jack wrote a lot of music for us. It was a fabulous experience and now, whether I am playing classical music or jazz music, the chamber music setting is what I prefer. Music that you can see through and is meant to be listened to without being in the distraction of a club or bar.

11. Your classical career has been really varied over the years, could you mention some highlights? Any favorite music that you played with the Long Beach Opera?

My classical career was, and is, mostly chamber music. My 10 years with the Long Beach Opera were great. I started on 3rd oboe for the classics and as the group started doing more modern pieces under its new leader, I switched to 1st clarinet. Two of the highlights were doing *The Ring* with a cut-down orchestra. It almost killed all of us, as we performed it with no subs on a Saturday and Sunday, all four operas. The other favorite was for chamber orchestra and was the story of Anne Frank. Just one singer and about 12 musicians. Great music and wonderful performances.

12. Do you have a preferred horn to play? I understand that you have concentrated on the oboe family. Does the oboe require more attention (practice) than the other horns?

The oboe is a full-time job. Reeds are a constant thing to deal with because the reeds actually serve as both sides of a mouthpiece. Working on oboe reeds taught me a lot about how clarinet and sax mouthpieces work. The reeds change with the weather, so we are always working on reeds. It's part of the oboe experience.

Flute is the first instrument I usually practice every day. The nice thing about the flute is it has no reed . . . and the hard thing about the flute is that it has no reed. It's the only modern woodwind instrument we don't put in our mouths. We balance it under our lower lip. The embouchure and breath control is everything. But on the days that I am "on," it's a beautiful thing. I started on the clarinet, and many people think of me as a clarinet player. It's all about the tone on the clarinet (as it is with all instruments) and the technique like the flute must be kept on top of. The clarinet is tuned in 12th's instead of octaves, which makes it difficult in it its own way. My advantage was that I started on clarinet.

I did most of my movie calls on 1st clarinet and Dan Wallin, the recording engineer, loved my sound. I am very proud to say that when Dan retired, I bought the set of speakers that he mixed many movies with. Tim Simonec is a brilliant composer and orchestrator, and I did much of my movie work with him. Then there is the sax with its flexibility and sweetness. I love them all. The easiest one for me to give up would be the oboe. It's a lot of work to keep all the instruments ready all the time, and as I age, I seem to concentrate on whatever someone writes for me. The true joy of my life is that all the literature written for me, especially chamber music, has increased the literature available for future woodwind players. You can hear that in my CDs which have music largely written for me.

13. Is there a favorite soundtrack for a movie that you played on? Do you have a favorite studio gig that you could mention?

Ratatouille is the favorite soundtrack I have played on. So many mouse- or should I say rat-chase scenes, really virtuoso playing. Bobby Shulgold on flute was perfect on every take. Also, there was the first date that I played with the Kenton band playing Dee Barton's music. That was my first time in a studio, with a professional band, playing at Capitol Records, with its history of great artists. Every time I work there, it's like looking at the history of pop music in the 20th century.

14. How do you deal with the pressure involved with playing in the studios? Having to have all your horns (flutes, clarinets, saxophones, oboes) ready to play must take a tremendous amount of work. Have you ever gotten to the studio and seen a part and wondered *"How in the hell am I going to do this,"* and then when the instant came to play, it came off flawlessly?

I never worried much about pressure in the studio. Even though a take can cost a lot of money with a big orchestra, the money is not the problem, so multiple takes are generally accepted. My concern is always during live playing, where many times we only get one shot at it. The business here in LA rarely lets us do multiple performances unless we are in a pit situation. For concert work, especially chamber music, we get one chance to make it perfect or perhaps two or three chances if we are lucky. Every audience expects perfection from listening to so many perfect recordings. They don't realize that live playing is not quite like that. But live or recorded, when it is perfect musically, there is nothing like it.

15. Where did you meet your business partner, Rheuben Allen?

I have known Rheuben since he had The Sax Shop in Hollywood 40 years ago. Beside being the number one repair shop at the time, at one point he was the busiest Yamaha dealer in the U.S. He is still active in design and repair of instruments. Most recently he created the Kenny G soprano that's doing great in the marketplace. He also has a line of sax necks that are really good. He seems to be working on something new every time I see him.

16. How did you come about re-designing clarinet barrels and bells?

I could never find the feel, sound, or intonation I wanted on the clarinet, so Bill Stevens, the lathe master, and I, just started trying new designs based on what was around at the time and then altering the specs on our own products until we found what we were looking for.

Trial and error, with some great epiphanies along the way, which became obvious as we figured them out.

17. What were stock bells and barrels lacking when you were using standard equipment on your horns? Was that the sole reason that made you decide to go out there and explore the possibilities?

Most stock barrels were just a straight hole from one end of the barrel to the other end. Then some variations came along, mostly with the reverse taper but none of those fit what I wanted to feel or hear. Bill and I did a lot of adjustments to the inside of the barrel. Plus, after they are made, we play and tune them 3 times until I like the feel and the sound. As far as bells, they are like a stereo speaker, with every speaker sounding different based on the design. Most of the bellmakers were just making the same or similar tapers. We changed that radically, as well as changing the weight of the bell.

18. How did you go about designing The AV Clarinet? How many prototypes did you receive before you were satisfied with the results?

Our contacts in many Asian countries sent us clarinets, and we would send them information back on how we would like them altered. We are now very satisfied with the bore and keywork on the instruments we are getting. And I must say, the barrels on the AV clarinet are made to our specs and play very well too.

19. Is designing an on-going process that continues with you today?

Our design is set, though the Asian makers tend to listen to everyone and make changes as they go. We have to remind them that what we want is not to be changed by suggestions from others.

20. What are your future plans?

Record as much as I can, with classical and jazz CDs on the front burner. I am rehearsing with a great sax quartet that will most likely do some local concerts, and hopefully a recording of a saxophone quartet written by John Scott, who is another fine composer that I have a long-term relationship with in the film business. I am also rehearsing with a clarinet quartet that Rheuben Allen has run for many years, and that has a CD finished, waiting to be issued.

John Scott has written a clarinet quintet (with string quartet) and a saxophone quintet (also with string quartet) for me that I hope we get recorded in the next year or so. I have just finished recording a double CD of pop music that should be available no later than September 2018.

I already have three unaccompanied pieces for the classical CD recorded and am looking forward to including John's pieces...

I would also enjoy finding a few dedicated students ... and, of course, I love making clarinet and sax mouthpieces.... Life is very busy.

Why Practice?

WHY CALL IT PRACTICE?

The word **practice** can be frightening and tedious. Please feel free to substitute words like *study, examine, training, learning, investigating, improving, examine, rework,* or whatever word is palatable to you. Teachers should use these different words when talking to students. Perhaps, we should never use the word practice again. Pick different words and it may change how you look at the music you study.

To determine why and how long you should investigate, the first thing you need to decide is *what is your relationship with music?* What do you expect back from music? And are you, or can you, fall in love with music? Perhaps, this is the most important inspiration for learning.

Is music a social outlet for you? Do you want to play professionally? How about playing in a community band or chamber music with friends? Whatever it is, if you can understand what you want to do and commit to it, you can define your practice habits more easily.

I have written about this before, however a little reminder might be in order.

We are in a Music, Art, and Technology Renaissance like mankind has never experienced before. Schools like Julliard, Curtis Institute,

Colburn, and at least 20 other conservatories are creating symphonic clones…players with incredible musical technique, fully schooled in Standard Literature and ready for any position in a major orchestra. I wish I knew what was going on in Europe and around the world.

Berklee, North Texas State, Cal State Schools, and a variety of other schools *(plus of course Jamie Abersold and online sources)* are creating jazz virtuosos at an amazing pace. More music students in the public school systems have superior instruction and are even learning music theory in junior high school. That's something that would have not been even considered when I went to school. There is also an abundance of media music sources for one to develop a concept at every turn in the road.

Yet the music business is declining as an option to make a living. When a lawyer, doctor, or computer programmer doesn't know something, they get paid while they find out the answer. An amateur musician must know what is expected to be prepared before they go to a rehearsal or a concert. A professional must be pretty much spot on at every task or most likely won't work much again.

Where are all these well-trained musicians going to work/perform, or are they destined to teach more virtuoso youngsters? I can tell you for sure that those student musicians who practiced most will get the jobs over those that were not fully committed. That fact holds true in almost every profession, by the way. It is still possible for any student to sit at the top of the heap by just practicing on a regular basis. I don't have a crystal ball and don't know what the future holds for our art, but I do know that we are turning out more expert musicians than ever in the history of mankind, that's for sure.

So next, it would do you well to consider *why* you practice music. Do you want to become a professional performer, a well-versed amateur musician with opportunities to play and perform music? Do you just enjoy practicing for the sake of practicing? Is there a religious or spiritual aspect to being in the practice room? Or does practicing give you insight to life?

If you want to become a musician of any type, it requires some amount of practice.

Music becomes more enjoyable when we practice (woops, *investigate*), as it allows us to play music at a higher level and to interact with others who have done the same. That is the prize of practicing. We up our game, if you will. It's really thrilling to play something perfectly that we have been practicing, and especially at the perfect moment when we are interacting with other people.

So, let me say that if you have a private music teacher, it will give you more inspiration to practice than perhaps a schoolteacher, who is dealing with many students in a room with a myriad of personalities and abilities at the same time.

So, if you are going to play in the elementary school band, you owe it to your mates to have learned the material being studied.

If you are playing in the junior high school band/orchestra or the high school band/orchestra, you have more responsibility, as you are not just practicing unison or similar materials as in elementary school.

If you are performing at the college level, you may just want to be in the marching band for the camaraderie, but you still have the responsibility to learn your individual part. Or, you may be studying music in a more serious manner to be a teacher, performer, or in some other music related field.

These pre-professional activities really do require a serious commitment from every student to uphold the quality of the ensembles they participate in.

Are you going to play in an ensemble as an adult for enjoyment? Here again, the ensemble will only be as good as the weakest link.

So, what is your commitment to study?

As beginners, we are just trying to hold the instrument and get a sound. But as we progress, each new musical experience is a building block to the next thing we do. It's important to make sure that the building blocks are strong. And of course, the answer to that is some level of study on our musical tool(s) of choice.

Is music a sacrifice for you, or something to look forward to? If it's a sacrifice, most likely you will give up on music and some point and, as an adult, be able to say, "Oh, I played clarinet for a year and could play *Mary Had A Little Lamb.*"

So, to change *sacrifice* into *purposeful participation,* some decision must be made by each person about how much of their time they are willing to commit to practice. Practicing is about priorities, and you may have to adjust your schedule to make time to practice.

It is really all about mental attitude . . .

There are parents who commit their children to music, thinking it will keep them off the streets when combined with swimming lessons, karate, golf, football, or whatever other time-consuming activity they can provide for their children.

Chances are, the children of these parents won't take music seriously *(unless they become charmed)* as subconsciously the kids understand what is happening. With karate, swimming, and the like, one can just go to class and not really have to practice the discipline as just going to the class or "practice" will get the student to a certain level where they can enjoy the endeavor.

Music moves slower than the other "time consumers" and that is why it requires a study commitment. Music takes work to even get started and regular solitary commitment to improving.

Solitary is one of the keywords in practice. It is something we do alone or with a little supervision when available. So, we need to be comfortable enough with ourselves to be alone, or in some cases uncomfortable enough with ourselves not to want to be with other people. I have seen great musicians come from both of these places. Needless to say, it is better that we like ourselves. But that is not always possible.

Another interesting aspect of practicing is that as we confront each new tidbit of information, we may find the aspect of becoming proficient daunting. For that idea, I use one of my favorite phrases, **"Be happy where you are at while you are trying to get to where you want to be"** —well at least as much as possible. Music is for the long run.

So, what is your motivation to play music? I think the best motivation is to keep up with your colleagues so you can have the best musical experience possible. This will continue to motivate you.

My experience was taking private lessons and only practicing enough to get through the lesson. That was until 9th grade, when I heard a band and decided that music was what I was going to do for a living. It was early enough in my life for me to make a commitment, and to understand what I wanted to do in life, but it ensured my success in starting serious practice time early. In my era that worked. In this new world, I think it may take even more commitment.

I think with commitment comes motivation. I like to say it doesn't make any difference *how much* you practice every day but it's the fact you do it on a *regular basis* that makes it successful.

Parents, you need to talk to your children about commitment once the decision has been made to pursue an interest in music. The commitment might not last forever and sometimes it ebbs and flows, however, it's important the student understands the concept of commitment.

For those of us who have committed to practice, it is a lifetime duty. As soon as one knows their level of commitment, the easier it is to institute a practice schedule. And it is all about schedule to get it done. One way for the student to have commitment is to have them pay for a portion of the lesson no matter how small the contribution is.

We all have different lifestyles as youngsters, we may have a large family or a family committed to many things. This can make it more difficult to find the solitude to practice.

When we are off to higher education, we must learn in every subject, but we still must be committed to practicing and playing with others as much as possible. As college students, we have no excuse for not adjusting our schedules to find time to practice.

As adults, however, we may now have our own family and getting time for solitude and practice every day may be difficult.

There are personal time clocks. Some people feel better in the mornings and some people feel good at night and there are many variations of relative mental and physical strength.

The best time to practice if your body allows it, is early in the day. It improves your whole day knowing you did your mental music exercise. The rest of the day is left for other commitments and hopefully playing music with some friends or colleagues. That's the simple way.

Otherwise, you will have to set up a practice schedule. Until practice becomes a daily habit, it's best to write down on a piece of paper your practice schedule and work it in with your schedule of other events and commitments. Put that piece of paper where you can see it. AND DO IT EVERY DAY. Take one day off a week and don't take your instrument on vacations. That is time for reflection, which can be as important as practicing.

There is always a reason not to practice.
It is incumbent upon us to find the reasons we
must practice and to find the time to do it.

Remember again, it is the *commitment* of practicing more than the *amount* of time you practice, so really aim for every day. If you are committed to being in one of the higher echelons of music, you will have to gradually increase your practice time and at one point in your life commit to a couple years of long hours of practice. Yet once again, it is the *habit* of practicing that makes this all happen. So, in the beginning, just make sure you engage music almost every day.

As in practice in the morning, practicing at the same time every day is very helpful in a successful practice schedule. The important thing is getting time in every day.

Remember that committed listening is part of practicing. If you know what it's supposed to sound like, it's much easier to latch on to the concept. Sit down to intentionally listen. Listening both with a score and without one is an important aspect of music study. In addition, have ambient music around you that is what you are studying. It all sinks in a little as you get used to the sound.

Practice being a better listener. Listen to be a better listener. Listen to yourself as you practice. Listen to your peers. Listen to experts in your field. Remember performing music is outgoing, listening is incoming, and sometimes we need to do both at the same time.

Listening is practicing and can be done anytime just by paying attention. Professional musicians often talk about an artist or colleague that has "big ears."

Here is a simple but doable practice routine.

1. Play the piece all the way through the best you can.
2. Start at the beginning and learn the first phrase. Start slow (as my friend Gerry Schroeder says, *"Tempo de Learno"*) and after you can play it slow, *gradually* increase the tempo.
3. Learn the second phrase in the same manner.
4. Play the first and second phrases together.
5. Go on like this though the whole piece playing a couple of phrases at a time.
6. Play the piece all the way through by concentrating on seeing the notes.

You will find as long as you can see the notes, you will be able to play the piece you have chosen. If you go blind for a second or so, go back and practice the difficult part again slowly.

To recap and to add a couple of thoughts: You need to practice. Anything you can't play should be learned slowly first and then gradually sped up, or better yet memorized. Dedicated listening is part of practice. Record yourself occasionally so you hear yourself from another perspective. Ask your teacher to play for you so you can hear how your part should be performed. Practice listening to yourself *while* you play

Oh, I am only 77 years old. I had better go get on with my study tonight.

We always make time for things we want to do.

On the Road (Again)

In my days on the road, we rode in what amounted to a Greyhound bus. We seldom flew, as by the time we got all our equipment checked in and picked up ground transportation, it was almost always easier just to stay on the bus even if it added hours to the trip.

Before *my* road stint with big bands, the band members would often drive in several cars, but this was gradually given up for the sake of having the whole band together. Mind you, these buses were *not* the motor coaches that we see these days with beds, living rooms, and even showers.

So, the current modes of transportation are cars, buses, coaches, railroads (not so much these days), and flying. In your journeys, there will be in heat, cold, wind, rain, snow, dirt and every environment you can think of.

Whether you're playing with a lounge band, as an opening act, a band trying to forge a name, a big band, a celebrity group, a symphony, a chamber music ensemble, a country western band, or a soloist, there is one constant...

...*the road is the road.*

It's a reality of the music business: *Sometimes in their lives, most musicians end up on the road, going to places known and unknown.* It may be to start a career, to maintain a career, to perform with a well-known celebrity; it may be *being* the celebrity, or it may end up becoming a permanent lifestyle.

I'm not talking about driving between 2 and 4 hours, doing the job, and then traveling back home with no rest, which may be a common scenario in many cities today.

So, what is it all about?

What it's all about is that you are not at home and you don't have the normal creature comforts that make life easy. This is much easier for young people than for older people. The road is difficult, in that the big routine is getting to the job, dealing with the time off, and getting to the next job.

Until you get off the road that's what you do.

There are big cities, little towns, military bases, state fairs, schools, concert halls, country clubs, and many other places to perform—and lots of territory to cover.

With all the negatives of being on the road, there are some beautiful places you will visit that other people pay good money to go see, and you'll meet some great people. When traveling or working is not the centerpiece of your existence, it's important to enjoy the *good* parts of being on the road, of which there are many.

So even with mostly work, there is still the opportunity to enjoy many sights that few get to see. In some cases, your significant other may be able to come meet you and enjoy the sights if you stay in one place long enough.

There are plenty of stories to be told of just getting to the job and finding a decent place to sleep, and perhaps even some decent food. There is always a new story to tell, and always boredom to deal with.

The big deal is to do your best not to hurt yourself on the road. Be moderate with food, alcohol, drugs (even for performance anxiety), and your daily routines. Walk slowly into new situations and pay attention to your environment. Find a way to get some exercise whether it means just walking or visiting the hotel pool/health club.

Most of all, do your very best to be kind to those on the road with you, and with those people you meet on the road. Try not to let personalities ruin your time or anyone else's time.

For those of you who end up on the road for long periods of time, remember that it's very difficult to maintain a marriage or relationship of any kind when you are away from those you care about. Your shared life together is going to be different while on the road, for both you and your significant other. You will both be leaning on new people for support since you won't be together. There have been many divorces because of extended road work.

Let's talk about health for a moment. When you are on the road, if you break a bone, *you are still on the road*. If you get a cold or the flu, *you are still on the road*. If you drink too much, *you and your hangover are still on the road*. You still go to work anyway. If you have a heart attack or some other serious injury, you will be in a hospital on the road while your group keeps going while looking for someone to take your place. And make sure you're fully "road ready" before you commit to returning, for your own sake and for the sake of your group. Some people have died on the road.

I was once on the road with a ballet company that did several performances a week. We had one truck with two crew members who had to set up the stage with props, take them down, drive to another city, and put them back up again. At one point, we had several performances in a short period of time, and one of the crew died from exhaustion. That's the road at its worst.

Your Agent/Manager is a very important element of your road experience:

- Do they over- or under- book you? It's much easier to book weekend days and holidays etc., so are they sensitive to the weekly fill-in dates as it affects your income and comfort? *Most fill-in dates pay less.*

- Do they consider the logistics of your travel and the time it takes to recuperate from that travel?

- Do they know of hotels close to where you are going to perform that work well for your rest and budget?

- Do they think of you as a valuable asset or just a group that makes money for them?

- Do they make clear the contents of your contract and what is expected from you?

- Do you have copies of the contract as well as your equipment rider so there are no questions between you and the employer when you arrive at a job?

- Does your contract have a clear paragraph on what happens if the terms of the contract are not met? Is the agent/manager a good liaison between the employer and your group?

- Do you have an agency that only books you or do they help you save money and facilitate a retirement and partnership plan if appropriate? Whether at home or on the road, there is no success without saving your money.

- Do you have an agency that always books a non-stop flight whenever possible, especially when airports like Chicago can get snowed in during the winter and are subject to storms in the summer? The last thing you need to slow you down is missing a connecting flight.

Your responsibility on the road is to basically show up as early as you can to alleviate the worry of the promoter and to perform at your best. There are always variables to playing your best, especially if you are performing mostly the same literature every engagement. I have found that sometimes when the band was the most tired, we played our best, as we had to summon extra energy to get the job done.

Be sure to treat the audiences and the local promoter as friends, in addition to all those who are helping you. Be nice to everyone you run into, because, like it or not, there is a reason for every job, even if you're not sure what it is at the time.

It's important to dress as professionally as you can and still be comfortable. Remember, at some level all road musicians are celebrities to someone. And need I say it, but I will. Always arrive with your best attitude and clear eyes and clean fingernails.

Remember that a bar is still a bar, whether a drink is $3 or $20, and a bed is a bed no matter what you are paying for the room.

And when you get home, your own shower and your bed feels ever so good.

It takes strength to play an instrument,
but a different strength than you might think.

Why You Should Record Yourself

The simple answer is to hear your own progress and to play your recording for others who may enjoy it. To record yourself is to know yourself or at least a lot more about yourself and your approach to music.

Keeping a recorded journal of yourself (audio or video) on a regular basis is a wonderful way to hear yourself improve over the months and years. It's also a reflection of what was happening at different points in your life. It's a tremendous learning tool that was not easily available until relatively recently. Save those recordings!!!

In the beginning, it's a way to give joy to other people, whether it is your parents, your friends, a concert audience, or anyone else. In the long run, it is your business card, as well as a catalyst for your career goals.

When I started there was no videotaping. It was 78, 45 and 33-1/3 RPM records and one had to invest in an expensive audio recorder to hear themselves play. As the years went on it was easier and easier to be able to record oneself, until now you can go into almost any big store and find some type of audio or video recorder. High-quality handheld recorders (no longer with tape) are available at any music specialty shop and on the Internet for a very reasonable price. In addition, with a good microphone, you can find recording programs for your computer from free to professional quality depending on your needs. You also get a hint at becoming a recording engineer while learning to record yourself and ultimately your friends.

You can also buy inexpensive devices to video yourself while recording sound at the same time. And of course, video recording is the standard these days. People seem to want to see you play as well as hear you. I have always wondered about the idea of listening with our eyes.

Either way, these recordings become the scrapbook of your life.

A word of caution! Whether you are recording yourself (either by audio or video), remember that it's the first "take," the one that is unedited, that shows who you really are—that is how you really play. Editing is for perfection and as we know nothing, or relatively nothing is perfect, never confuse your raw recording and your edited recording in judging where you are really with your playing. In listening to recordings of others, keep in mind whether it was **To record yourself is to know yourself.** "live" or perfected in the editing booth. It will make you feel a lot better to contrast yourself to live recordings (not common in recent years), as you will not be assuming that you are supposed to sound perfect every time and to put that huge chain around your neck. Remember there is a lot of humanity in music. Be kind to yourself.

Music is huge. Ask any great concert violinist in the world if they can play a good country fiddle behind a singer. Most likely not. Both kinds of music are valid. All music is valid despite our own concepts and tastes and the concepts of those that create music.

There is a blog called *Jazz on the Tube*. It comes out every day with a video, mostly of great jazz masters. The creator of the web show recently asked for any information his listeners may have about great jazz players he does not know about. Then he said, "There seems to be as many great players as stars in the sky." Be sure and accept your place in the galaxy of music and know that it's important despite all the other stars in the sky. Your star could prove to be very important for you and others. We never know nor should we judge ourselves by comparing ourselves negatively to others. We all bring something special to the music. Ourselves.

Make your music fun, not work, and understand that though music is time-consuming, it's not difficult, it's just the speed of the river, and we will always grow and get better and own more of the galaxy of music, just by practicing a bit.

Back to recording for just a moment. It changes every day and there are more opportunities to see and hear it daily, even with the chance of harm to live music. Remember, live music is unique in its sound, its presentation, and its importance.

I don't know where recorded music is going, but I do know it will continue to change and be here for a long time, so use it wisely and to your advantage by paying attention to it.

#29

The Importance of Repetition

Unless you were born with or developed perfect pitch and perfect recall, or something close to it, you will most likely have to learn music like most of us do. By repetition.

From the beginner to the Master of Music, that is how we learn music. Usually in this order:

1. Try to play the music all the way through.

2. Go back and try to play the music all the way through slowly and notice the problem areas.

3. Start at the beginning and play the first phrase *very slowly* (you must be able to see the notes, to play the notes).

4. Gradually, and perhaps with a metronome, increase the speed slowly (one more click of the metronome) to get the first phrase up to speed.

5. Learn the next phrase the same way.

6. Put the two phrases together (you will most likely have to slow down a bit) and work until you can play both phrases together at the tempo you want.

7. Keep doing this until you have learned the whole piece.

8. Play the piece a few times and enjoy your commitment to excellence.

It's like learning to talk when you are a small child. We learn by saying back to our parents what they say to us. Repetition!!!

Having laid this method out, realize that when you come back the next day you most likely won't be able to play it perfectly, and you may have to go through the whole process again, either a phrase at a time or with the whole piece. This time it will be a little easier. Keep doing this until you own the music.

Repetition is not only something we do with the music, but also something we do on a daily basis. So, repetition is repeating what you practice from day to day, as well as repeating it as a way of practicing.

Some people serious about practicing a piece of music will play it until they feel comfortable playing the music from the page. Others will memorize it. Either way the ultimate goal is to take the music off the page and own it in your soul—so it does not sound like you are reading music, but that the music is coming from within you…or the universe.

What I have described is learning music by reading it from a page and looking at it.

There are some people who learn another way—by listening to music, and then trying to play it on their own instrument. That is called learning *by ear*. However, though they don't read music, the learning process is much the same. They imitate what they hear on a recording of some sort until they have learned it. It's easier for these people to make the music sound like it's coming from inside themselves because they skipped the exercise of reading the music first.

If you repeat something long enough, sooner or later it will be memorized to your delight, and without the written music, you have a better chance of sounding like the music came from your soul.

I am not suggesting that you must memorize everything you practice. However, in preparation for learning tunes, or a concerto, which are usually performed by memory, why not memorize something occasionally along the way so it's not a surprise when you become an advanced player. The act of memorizing will improve your ability to listen.

Most instrumentalists learn the reading way. If you learn enough pieces this way, you gradually learn to play the music as if it's coming from your soul while you are sight-reading the music.

You must be able to see the notes, to play the notes.

I was fortunate in the way I was taught. I learned the clarinet first; then after several years took up the saxophone. After another several years I took up the flute, and finally the oboe. In the meantime, I was messing around with the recorder. In each case, I had to start from the very beginning with long tones, whole notes, half notes, eighth notes, and then sixteenth notes, etc. I went through the exercise books to train my fingers and the literature to get up to speed on what was required of me. So, each time I picked up an instrument I learned to approach music again from the beginning.

For the beginner, this is all more difficult than for the advanced player, as they are not only trying to learn music, but they are also trying to learn an instrument too. They need to think about holding a foreign object, perhaps how to breathe, to do the muscle building for holding the instrument and creating an embouchure, and to learn how to find the right movement for their fingers. All of that can be a slow and arduous task. After many years of playing, performing, and practicing, these are still all concerns of mine, and I am looking for constant improvement.

I always advise the beginning student to practice slowly and learn how to listen to their notes and their body. They simply can't practice as long in the beginning because there is so much to learn, and so many muscles to train. The answer to this dilemma is to include dedicated listening to improve their concept, and find, or revive, the love of a finished piece of music. Also practicing in shorter time periods, a few times a day, rather than forcing improvement seems prudent.

Work on practicing one minute a day. Let the problems of the day—the things that are pulling on us, the procrastination, and all the other little things that make it difficult for us to approach our instrument—go away. Pick up the instrument and play until you are tired. In the beginner's case, that may be a few one-minute sessions. For the more seasoned player, it gets to be longer study times. For those who can't afford the one minute a day, don't really want to do it anyway. It is work—and there is solitude in learning. As Jack Wheaton used to say, "learning is a painful process."

It doesn't have to be painful with only a minute a day (or more). Your instrument can charm you, and that is the beauty of music. Get a little better with repetition, and know that repetition will yield results, and that makes us feel good.

Selling and Music

So, you may ask yourself what does selling and music have in common? Perhaps more than you think.

We call it the music business, so it seems like we are either selling ourselves, our store, our studio, or something like a CD, music track, or DVD. Do you learn how to play music and then do all the business yourself? That depends on what you are selling.

Do you have a business plan like all other businesses? As a musician, a business plan may be a practice schedule and perhaps a plan on how to distribute your CDs or how to procure students. As a music store, it's an advertising plan along with a plan to contact schools. Your repair department might be part of your plan to get traffic to your brick-and-mortar store.

I don't know how it is in school these days, but the idea of money, how to use your money wisely, how to create a business model, how to sell, or any other kind of business class was not offered in high school or college through the music department.

As a musician, you must sell yourself. Perhaps you need representation if you are a soloist, featured act, or featured vocalist. Compare that with a side person who belongs to a group of people they work with on a regular basis.

You must sell your playing when you do an audition. If you record, you need to sell your recordings. Or do you sell an electronic track, a CD, a DVD, or all the above? If you are a composer, you may have to sell yourself to a director or music supervisor. Think about how many instances where you are in a situation where presentation (another synonym for selling) is paramount in getting a job or keeping a job.

Did you spend many years kind of heartlessly practicing, without committing to being the best you could be? Then if you became serious about being in the music world in some capacity, you had to sell yourself by committing to be all you could be. You had to sell yourself on and to yourself. You had to be the one responsible for your actions.

Through all the years of practicing and for the rest of your life in music sales, your mannerisms and presentation to the rest of the world become part of your selling ability. That is your ability to have a single person, or a large group of people, see or hear something your way. Or you must adjust your attitude to do everything you can to fill the purchasers' needs. In addition, those that represent you become part of your team and your persona.

At some level, everyone else is likely to be a salesperson too.

You must understand there are salespeople whose only purpose in life is to make a sale. They don't care what they are selling and they don't care what affect the sale will have on you. They will say anything to make a sale and they are usually tricky about getting you to buy what they are selling—especially if you don't know exactly what you want to buy. That is the difference between an honest sale—where each person comes out with something that makes them happy—and a "con job."

I have personally found that listening to people talk about their needs and desires is one of the best sales techniques to find out what a person wants to buy. A good salesperson will do their best to fulfill their needs or point the client to someone who can. Pointing them to someone more qualified to fulfill their needs is a wonderful sales technique that can give you many sales in the future. The buyer will appreciate your honesty. However, this is only after you have done everything in your own power to satisfy their needs, as the buyer may be inclined to stay with the person you recommended and forget your benevolence.

We have all seen a person that talks too fast and puts out a barrage of information on why we should believe something. As Dan Jacobs has reminded us, "Forcing or bullying a prospect will always generate resistance."

I think you understand the idea that much of what we say is selling, whether it be an idea or a widget. I think you also understand that honesty with oneself and others is paramount in selling or presenting.

However, let me remind you of one thing. Everyone you come across does not deserve your truth. So, keep your truth for the people who deserve it; and find a way to tell the others what you want to say, what they want to hear, in a way that doesn't offend them.

Most of us have fragile egos, so when selling to someone that has a different opinion than you, consider how you can make your point without bruising their ego. In some cases, you may realize you can't change someone's idea. That's acceptable too. You don't have to win every discussion or sell every widget in your bag.

What about selling a product to others? As far as selling products, I once again suggest you purchase both of Daniel Jacobs' books, *The Natural Laws of Selling* and *The Natural Law of Closing*. I could never cover the subject in this format as well as he does in his books, plus, he has a great way in which he tells you this information.

As far as selling yourself, your products, and what you do for others, some of the things I find make a difference are: your appearance, your truth, your history, your speech, your experience, your plan, your intent, your presentation, and your follow up.

What I want everyone that reads this to know is it's all about you, and the things that an observant person can tell by being with you. We can only be who we are, but by the same token we can always work on improving ourselves through the lessons we learn in life.

Some wisdom does come with age, if we pay attention and work on not repeating our mistakes. Much of what we believe is often not the truth. Becoming more truthful with ourselves, and others whenever possible, is the basis of wisdom. Along with this is knowing when not to speak and just listen.

The bottom line for me is that I must sell myself honestly to be happy. For me personally, that means accepting that I can't be great at everything and realizing what I am good at and what I can improve. That means taking charge of my practice time and in my case recordings and a little music contracting, as well as my teaching. What is your bottom line?

Perhaps someday we will discuss selling an instrument or that spare mouthpiece, or should I say your box of mouthpieces or whatever piece of musical equipment you are not using. I will say one thing about that now. The better the quality of the instrument you buy, the easier it is to sell. I can tell you, the market for $100 flutes that don't play well is not very good.

There are some people who will only buy the most expensive thing, others that will only buy something on sale, and yet others that will always buy the best product for the money. It's a philosophy they have learned from their life. Quality counts to me whenever I can afford it. And quality is usually cheaper in the long run.

> *I never keep score with my friends,*
> *until I really start losing.*
> —**Tony Gumina**

More Recording Adventures and iClassical-Academy.com

AM I NUTS? A RECORDING STUDIO?

I don't think we can say these are normal times. The Covid-19 virus is upon us and getting worse in many places. Politics are meaner and more contentious than they've ever been. Our ability as musicians to make a meaningful living has become increasingly difficult to maintain. In fact, a nurse that I know thinks this kind of living is going to be the new normal. We can all hope she is wrong.

So, what's the answer?

I don't know.

What I do know is many young musicians are using the new technology of music to try and even the playing field. Most musicians between 18 and 60 are building recording studios along with video capacity in their homes. They are putting parts down on other people's recording projects as well as producing their own projects. The cost of good recording equipment has come way down, so it makes sense to invest in technology. That may be the new normal, or there may be something we don't know about yet. However, since we don't know about the future, why not learn a technology that's available to us now and include it in your repertoire? I guarantee you, from what little I have tried, it will make you a better musician as it helps you listen and see yourself in a new way.

I am not a big fan of bands and vocal groups utilizing Zoom, as frankly after having seen one Zoom presentation, I wanted to listen to some music without having to focus on twenty or thirty musicians in tiny video boxes.

What I did since I was retired, well actually the last two weeks, is I went out and bought a recording rig (no video quite yet) to see what it was all about. My recordist for my past several projects, Tom Zink, suggested some equipment, which I bought. And when I got it all set up, I looked at it and said, "Now what"?

I was talking to my friend, Tom Kubis, who receives these email blasts and has had a studio in his home for many years. He suggested since my attitude was "now what," that I write in this blog about what my experiences are as I learn my new system. So that's what I am going to do occasionally. I can't tell you about everything because I am only learning one method. However, you can feel my joy and angst as I learn my system.

No matter what system you choose from the list below it will be good enough for a professional presentation. It's up to your budget and commitment. Of course, a pro studio means you are spending more time doing that than just improving your music and helping yourself stay in the business. So, don't forget to practice a minute a day.

There are four basic types of recording setups that are in use today. They are:

1. **Bedroom Studio**—typically a small setup next to your bedside and is the absolute minimum you need to record sound onto your computer.

2. **Dedicated Home Studio**—typically a room in your house used solely for recording that includes both studio furniture and acoustic treatment.

3. **Semi-Pro Studio**—can be either at your home or a different location, and typically includes the equipment necessary to record multiple musicians simultaneously.

4. **Pro Studio**—typically located at a commercial facility and includes whatever tools necessary to produce professional results in the most efficient way possible.

They all use a variety of computer interfaces to record. Most of my professional friends are using one of these three: Pro Tools, Logic, or Digital Performer. There are many other computer interfaces, though. And there are plenty of professionals and specialty stores that can help you decide what your needs are.

I chose Digital Performer, as it's one of the easiest programs to use and I did not see myself doing a lot of midi tracks for quite a while. I wanted to become fluent at recording myself and my friends live. I also have not considered video, even though that seems to be part of the new, self-made, entertainment model.

I bought books on the system and went YouTube crazy trying to get up to speed. The problem was the books were not very current and the YouTube videos went so fast that even if I watched them 20 times, I would still not have a clue. The video guys seem to assume that we novices know much more than we do.

I suggest private lessons. I have a friend and wonderful composer, Victor Vanacore, who had a specialist sit behind him for a week straight while he learned. Since I don't have that kind of cash, I think I am becoming a once or twice-a-week type of guy for lessons.

I thought my first lesson went well. I went through the basics of the computer screen and what most of the nobs, dials, and icons did— and thought I had a good understanding of what was going on. I took notes and made myself a cheat sheet on many of the keyboard short-cuts (which I suggest you learn) so I could work a little faster. I was feeling very good.

The next day I opened the program and nothing worked. My

teacher suggested a digital memory disk and he figured out what was wrong. We then went through setting up a project. It was becoming obvious to me that my equipment, especially my computer, might not be quite up to the task. It worked, but it worked SLOWLY. I also, with some help, figured out that there are many types of cables and that my regular USB cable system was going to work okay for my home system, which uses USB cables. But I found out that the more powerful equipment might require Firewire, Thunderbolt, Optical, or Ethernet (I'm sure there are more).

The very next day I opened the program and guess what. It didn't work again. So, Tom Zink, my teacher, decided it was best if we videotaped every lesson, *which is a great idea*. We went through most of the instructions again with a video that I could review daily, and that really helped.

He even made a template that I could open and do a "save as" that was repeatable for what I wanted to do. Which at this point was just to record an unaccompanied suite for clarinet that John Scott was writing for me. It went slowly, but well, and I even got a finished product—but of course not to my liking. I needed to be more particular about my own equipment like reeds mouthpieces and ligatures and realized that I was always playing with someone else and just adjusted to them. I noticed even the slightest slip-up seemed like a bomb going off. And now I had to play perfectly *and* pay attention to the recording too. Yikes! The good news was I only had to call Tom a couple of times.

Since then, I have gotten much faster that when something doesn't work, I can usually figure out what is wrong on my own and finish a movement of my new music. In the last few days, I was even able to start working faster and learn a couple of things by myself. I can't wait to see what Tom thinks of my own decisions. There are many issues in sound production.

I suggest to you that you buy the best equipment you can afford for the type of recording you are going to do . . . especially micro-phone(s) and speakers.

The best news is I think if I can be patient with the learning curve, I will be able to do this and learn from my mistakes.

Well, of course, there must be a P.S. or two. My friend Victor didn't like my reverb, so I messed with it and now everyone thinks it's better. The truth is, I created a file with no reverb on it—just one little button and I mean a little button.

Today I woke up and many of my files seem missing and the ones I have are not getting sound again. At least the program is loading. I am taking Tom Zink's advice and getting a solid-state internal hard drive for my old computer. It just arrived in the mail. It will make everything faster and easier to use. I guess it lets it breathe. The only thing I can say to you as I send this out is "two steps forward and one step back."

iCLASSICAL-ACADEMY.COM

I am happy to announce that I have entered into a contract, produced 9 videos, and delivered them, on the subject of The Business of Music, to iClassical-Academy. They are on the site now.

I want to thank Tom Zink for his outstanding video production, and his presentation advice for the videos.

www.iClassical-Academy.com is a world-class teaching resource for classical music. They utilize only the finest professional classical artists as teachers (you get to watch their private lessons with out-standing students), plus they deal primarily with solo classical litera-ture. For me, the best part is that the teachers not only advise the students, but they also demonstrate what they are saying. It's a new entry to high-end teaching of solo literature. You owe it to yourself to go to their website now and get acquainted with their excellent staff.

iClassical-Academy.com

It's well worth your money to see what the next generation of great musicians are learning. And the fees are reasonable. If you are a serious musician (even a jazz or pop musician), consider purchasing a lifetime membership, and as new teachers are added, you can advance your concept of classical music on a permanent basis.

Ongoing Experiences with My Home Studio

You have heard the expression, "if it can go wrong, it will?"

Well, the good news is, that despite the learning curve, I am learning the program and getting better at it. The bad news is, sometimes when I open the program it doesn't work. *At all*. Then I called my teacher, Tom.

So, more good news, my friend and world-class composer, John Scott, has written a suite of 14 movements called *Pentatonia*. And you guessed it . . . all the pieces are written based on the pentatonic scale for unaccompanied clarinet. It's so artistically composed you will likely not notice it is based on a 5-note scale. He has also composed a suite of 7 pieces for solo alto saxophone.

"In the Mountains"

1. Sunrise
2. In the Mountains
3. Clear Water Stream
4. In the Cave.
5. The Eagle
6. Deep Slalom
7. Sunset between Two Peaks

What a wonderful way to learn how to record single instruments.

I haven't started the saxophone suite yet. However, *Pentatonia* is going so well with my equipment, I am planning to make a CD of it, and I am sure "In the Mountains" will be on that recording also. Of course, I will have to redo the first few Pentatonias as the distance from the microphone is not always the same, I didn't understand the plug-ins and I wasn't as careful to make them as near perfect as I could, as I was only thinking of it as a recording lesson.

The truth is, recording myself daily is the best "music" lesson I've ever had. I wish I'd started recording 50 years ago. I listen to myself much more carefully now. I found I have plenty of friends who have been doing this for many years to advise me on the shortcomings of my recording technique.

I had a total blow up and lost all my masters, which thankfully Tom was able to retrieve. I have learned, or should I say, re-learned, to always back up. ALWAYS!!!

It seems that Digital Performer likes the more stable internal drive, so a rework of the system is in order. The good thing is the computer I use is dedicated to recording. So, I am going to convert my internal CD drive to a Blue Ray drive for back up and will also have the digital external drive. A CD drive will be added to the hub which will give me the ability to listen to CDs on my great set up and speakers (thanks to Sweetwater and Dan Wallin) or import music in CD format.

I like learning slowly and practicing for more perfection, so I think it will be many months before I start with the midi section of the program. I'm so happy with the microphone and Motu interface, as they are relatively easy to use.

I expect problems here and there, and of course, to make mistakes, but it seems I am on a solid footing to improve quickly.

These Times We Live In

So, we have COVID-19!

Most auditoriums are shuttered and festivals are minimized, as are jazz and other music venues. Instrumental conferences are mostly over Zoom. We must face the fact, the disease is likely not to end soon.

So, what do we do?

Don't just wait to see what happens. Stay Active!!!

Find a way to play and get paid. Start a porch concert on your front porch and invite the neighbors, and ask one of them to pass the hat. Pick the same day every week and block off the street if you can. The audience can sit on your lawn, properly distanced, or in the street or across the street.

Try and get with an institution that sells tickets for online concerts. Or figure out a way to do your own video concerts and get paid or ask for a donation to a PayPal account.

Make recordings, DVDs, and sound files. Get them out to the public. People are staying home, so we must go to them if they can't come to us. I had a friend that sent out a message on social media that said he had a new CD. His intention was to sell 100 and if he sold those, he would make 100 more. It was a simple package with a cardboard sleeve with his picture on the front and the names of the tunes on the back (his tunes). It was a fantastic Latin Jazz presentation too. That's just one idea. If you have money, you could even hire a publicist or some other person to help you sell.

Another idea is to stream your music. Don't panic, that just means to videotape a performance or a finished rehearsal. Then get an institution to play it or sell it as a DVD. An institution might even produce the video for you. The 92nd St. YMCA (92Y) in NYC puts on a streaming classical video series, as do many other Jazz and Classical entities. Try *Jazz on the Tube* or *Chamber Music America*, which has a streaming directory, or whomever you can think of to create or play your stream. Remember that many people listen with their eyes. And in fact, that's even an important part of a live performance.

We all only want to play music, write music or words, or do our kind of visual art. We really don't like to do the work to sell our efforts—in most instances. But take an hour every day and promote yourself or your group or your whatever. Or you can do your music and art, and do it again and again, and not sell anything. At least you are doing what you want—if you can afford it.

But for those in the business of music, sales are a requirement. You can make that happen. You must ask for the money!

A word of caution: Make sure you get clearance for any music or work that is under copyright protection.

Do something even if it doesn't work. We all love live music, but whether live or recorded, it's important to keep creating and keep your art in the community. And once again, I remind you don't forget to ask for money. You are a professional.

With the sad news that Columbia Artists has closed its doors, it is vital to perform in some way. The dumbing down of the world, along with the COVID-19 virus will look the other way and forget us if we don't persevere. We can't help that only a minority of people understand what the arts bring to them. So, we must scream until they hear us.

We don't know what the musical and artistic landscape will be post-COVID-19, but there will be something. Some of you on the cusp will find other work because it is necessary. Those who are left will mostly have to adjust to a new way of thinking. I suggest you look forward and see how you can reinvent yourself and your music.

CAREER GOALS

I want to talk for a moment about something I feel is important. It's about opportunity and persistence.

One of my favorite concert pianists grew up with a father who was also a concert pianist and a mother who was a piano teacher. She started studying at the age of 3 and gave her first recital at the age of 6, which was very good. She now has many recordings and is busy with recitals, and symphony concerts.

That is the ideal scenario to become a concert artist. However, most of us don't have that opportunity! So how do those of us that came to music in a more random form pull off a solo career or *any* career in music?

Desire and persistence!!!

My desire and persistence.

My parents worked for a steel company, and though not rich, we had a good life. My music experience was private lessons from 4th grade on. Our only recorded music source was AM radio and Perry Como 78 recordings (he was a former barber turned crooner with a television show in the late 50s and early 60s). We never even thought of live performances. There were 5 television stations, 1 Classical radio station, no jazz stations, and lots of 50s R&R and Country Western Music until I got into high school. I studied with a private teacher who worked at the local music store and worked at the local Civic Light Opera until I went to college.

College is when my serious study began. My father died from cancer the week after my high school graduation. My mother told me she would do whatever she could to help me but advised me not to hurt myself, you know, doing all the things young men like to try. My relationship with her was what most likely kept me from hurting myself. The best start in life is, of course, to have great parents. Which I did.

Do you see where I am going with this?

By the time I was in my junior year of college, I had finally developed a deep love of music. All music, classical, jazz, pop, etc.

Though my musical education was mostly classical, I had good teachers in college and continued my studies until I was well into my thirties. I still study today. I guess we never quit trying to be better at our craft. We aim at perfection when very little in life is perfect. With the current COVID-19 crisis, it's an opportunity for me/us to get back to basics and tighten up techniques that slipped a bit when working. Also recording the fourteen movements of John Scott's *Pentatonia* for unaccompanied clarinet hasn't hurt either. And now I have just finished the 8 unaccompanied saxophone pieces entitled "Alpine Suite."

The years in my life between 20 and 65 were jobs I loved, jobs I hated, and even jobs I was not qualified for. And I usually never felt quite qualified enough, though I really was. But I did not let fear keep me from playing music, *ever*. And now when I listen back to my early recordings, I love them. I learned on the job. Two things I really enjoyed were playing baritone sax with Stan Kenton and solo clarinet on *Ratatouille* and other Pixar movies. Also, 10 years with the Long Beach Opera helped hone my skills. My Chamber Music Trio "Musique" was the highlight of my life.

Throughout all those years since I left college, I played in chamber music ensembles and orchestras; did solo performances, opera, jazz bands, and anything else I could do to play the music I really loved. I even spent 10 years only playing for fun while I was an entrepreneur in the entertainment industry. After 65 it was more music and fewer jobs.

My point is this.

Whether you get to start early and have the opportunity, or you start later in life and have to carve out a niche for yourself, or even if you take a very bumpy road to success, the secret is a commitment to a standard of excellence, and not to give up when the hurdles come.

One must only have the desire, the will, and spend the time to stay with music. *It starts by practicing one minute a day.* See where that takes you. If you belong to music, it will embrace you and at the very worst, if you can't make a living, you will have found a new love.

So . . . What Do We Do Now?

We certainly don't know what the landscape will be like after COVID-19. So, it seems to me like a good time to improve our own playing, learn new literature, and polish the rough edges of our technique. To put it simply, it's time to practice our crafts with a zeal that we may have lost.

It's also time for introspection. Time to learn the truth about ourselves and the world around us. When do we have such a chance as this free time we have now? We can worry about the future . . . or plan for the future. So, let's plan on how to be better musicians or artists. Let's plan so that no matter what comes in the aftermath of this pandemic, we have new or stronger tools to deal with the reality to come.

For younger students, especially the ones doing homeschooling, I urge you to do something different if you aren't already doing it. First, stay away from television, computer games, etc. as much as possible. Instead, use the Internet to investigate the many things that may interest you. You can always get tutoring on your instrument, learn instrument repair, learn sound design . . . or you can learn to build a fence or just examine any subject you even think you might be interested in . . . and there will be a video you can watch. All of that is on YouTube as well as the Internet in general. That might even take you to the library to read up on one of your interests. This time of COVID-19 is a great time to invest in or create your interests. If you don't have an interest, this is the time to find one. Time goes so much faster when we are involved in something positive.

Let's talk about what is happening now and what we can do for ourselves to improve our own situation, and hopefully the situation of others. Let's talk about truth and beliefs.

I am saying the following for myself . . . and proffering it to you:

Almost everything we see on mass media, i.e., motion pictures, streaming events, and television is an edited event (including television news). Which means the truth has been edited to fit someone's vision or to manipulate the viewer.

Social media (the Internet and Internet chat sites) is a lot of people giving their opinion on whatever the topic of the day is. Most always it is personal and only sometimes factual. Musical recordings are edited to make the music sound perfect, with no mistakes, perfect blend, and perfect sonic qualities.

The print media is run by executives that want to see their vision of the world mirrored in their newspaper. Some actual reporting does take place, but depending on the narrative, one often must read in between the lines to get the truth from the statement.

People come up with their own opinions partially based on early childhood teaching from their parents and opinions from those contemporaries they grow up with. Many of these learning sources must be examined to get the truth. We all have opinions, but how do we know it's the truth?

As television police inspector Jack Friday used to say, "Just the facts ma'am, just the facts."

So, we have all these opinions based on edited events in our life, and teachings that in some cases may be faulty, yet they may seem beautiful or even righteous. This is one of the dilemmas of our time and in some cases, family history.

It becomes important for us to remember that much of our current influences are edited events. It is our job to see the truth through the edits.

We must learn to cast aside opinions and see the truth of our own experiences and what may be manipulating us. It seems we must experience life firsthand and let our own experiences and insights be our truth. We must pay attention and always ask ourselves what we are really taking into our souls. What is the truth of any situation?

That's a question we must ask ourselves in this time of COVID-19 while we have the time to ask ourselves. We must slow down and think a little more.

There is a little problem, however. It's difficult to change our habits, by depending on other people's experiences, prejudices, opinions, and edits. I have heard many times before that "learning is a painful process."

One of the quotes I included in my journal says:

With great pain comes great change.
If you are not ready for change,
then you are not in enough pain.
—Anonymous

We can still enjoy frivolous things…and just remember that's what they are—a respite from the truth. We can also do things we enjoy for the sake of doing them. Relaxation time and time to reflect is not a luxury but rather is mandatory to refresh our mind and experience new thoughts. How can we experience anything new if we are on a treadmill all the time?

Let's all remember that's why we go to "live" concerts and events, and once this terrible infection is a thing of the past, it is my hope that the live experience becomes more important than ever.

PHILANTHROPY

I have heard there are 50 million people in the United States that are hungry and must utilize food banks. The food banks are so overwhelmed they must ration the amount of food they give to families. If you have a little money to spare (or a lot of money), please consider giving it to a local food bank, as your help is really needed now. You will feel good that you helped a neighbor.

INSPIRATION

We have all come to music in a unique way. It could have been years of playing around with it and not being serious, and then one day realizing what an important part of life music is for us. Or it could have been a "Zuethian" Thunderbolt that struck us down with the realization that our lives had just changed . . . for better or worse. And of course, there are many variations to those two examples or even something completely different. At any rate, our future has changed. So how do we keep the inspiration to keep on practicing and improve on a regular basis? We live in a musical Renaissance like the world has never known, and with that, there are so many ways to experience music and learn new things.

We have recordings, videos, radio, television, live concerts, clinics and seminars, and the computer and Internet with its myriad of informational sites, some of which allow us to record ourselves, or even play along with accompaniment from a website, *bla bla bla*. I am sure that's just some of the possibilities we can access.

So how do we turn all these opportunities into inspirational moments?

Just like when we practice and sound leaves us, we should look for opportunities to search out sources that inspire us and bring music or great thoughts to us.

My most recent inspiration is Hillary Hahn on LinkedIn. This three-time Grammy award winner is doing a series of 100 days of video of her practicing. What a great opportunity and inspiration to hear such a mature musician practicing just like we do. Start slow and work on the music until it's in the fingers, and then move the tempo up until the music is playable up to speed.

What an inspiration to hear that brave woman not sounding her best, showing us her frailties to let us all see how practicing is done.

I have always believed that music teachers should take a piece of music they can't play and take a whole lesson from time to time to show and remind the students of the world how practicing is done. Practice for your student. It's time-consuming. That's what students seem to not understand. It's time-consuming for every musician in some way. There is no shortcut to learning.

Playing fast and hoping is not the answer. Playing the piece through, identifying the difficult phrases, practicing slowly and gradually increasing the speed with a commitment to learning the hardest parts of a piece of music until we own it, is the answer I know. When we finally own it completely, we can relax a bit and not criticize ourselves so much. We can turn off the internal dialogue and just play. But that takes time and a regular commitment to practicing. I am not talking about the musicians who have perfect recall and perfect pitch who may approach practicing differently. I have a feeling there is a routine they must go through that is time-consuming in some manner too. Only a few geniuses every few generations get a free ticket, as they seem to have been born having practiced in the ether.

For me, music is some type of religion, so I am always looking for inspiration. Just as a true believer practices their religion on a regular basis, so must a musician. And as with practicing, which is time-consuming, so is chasing inspiration. I say don't wait for your inspiration; rather seek it out. It's easy to find and yes, it's time-consuming. That's the blessing of it all.

Ownership

My last article was about inspiration. So, once we are inspired, how do we own music?

I see it as having the music and the technique in our hands. Not our mind. To achieve that thought requires repetition in our practice. Not a little repetition but a lot of it. Starting slow, using a metronome, and working at making our body work in a non-injurious and relaxed way. Trying to avoid adopting bad habits when learning the scales, études, or works of music. Remember, if we learn the music in an imperfect way, that is how we will always play it.

We use our minds when thinking about what to do. Posture, seeing the notes, and understanding that even scales are music and not exercises is a big plus. Whether we are memorizing something or reading from the page the idea is to get the music off the page. It helps if we treat our practice as if an audience is listening to us.

For students of all ages, an excellent teacher is important. For those who are out of school and no longer taking private lessons, it's even more important to not ignore any imperfection in our practice. The mind and then the body remember what we learn whether it was correct or imperfect.

It's important that we arrange our study sessions to include scales, études, and repertoire (whether the repertoire is learning tunes or learning concertos, or any other music intended for the public).

Scales are the building blocks—and it starts with the chromatic scale, which is the alphabet of music. Few students understand the chromatic scale and the idea of half steps as the basis of most of the music we play. So that becomes something that the beginner seems to learn slowly and only after several years. Once they know the chromatic scale, it's important to do exercises based on this scale. Then come the major, minor, augmented, and diminished scales along with the many modes from other countries.

Though we may play from music or tunes that we have learned, it's important to memorize scales. Try starting scales as whole notes, half, quarter, etc. Starting with whole notes not only makes it easier to memorize the scales, it allows us to study our hands and body to ensure that only the parts of the body that have to be used in a certain way are doing their job and everything else is very relaxed. Remember, fast is relaxed, not only in the hands, but in every other aspect of our body.

Next, we have the études, which generally work on a certain problem we encounter on our instruments. But make no mistake, études are music as much as they are a study of something. Always play scales or études musically.

Again, start slowly with your metronome and gradually increase the speed. If you increase the speed and start making mistakes, slow the metronome down to the previous speed and don't go faster until your fingers know the patterns they must learn. Make sure fingers, forearms, shoulders, and neck are relaxed and your breath is smooth and not forced.

Repeat the difficult parts more than anything else. I like to play the piece through, work on the problems and then play the piece again. That isn't the end. The next day we may still not feel comfortable with our study, but chances are it will be a bit better. We keep doing that daily until we own the notes and the music.

Most soloists, whether they are classical, jazz, country, swing, ethnic, etc. play by memory. Those in smaller groups, for example, a string quartet, aren't expected to play by memory. However, in the past few years, I have seen chamber groups of all types playing by memory. The point is, whether we are playing by memory or reading music, we must take the music off the page and make it our own.

So, in making the music something we own, how much liberty should we take with phrasing marks and tempo, etc.? These are all things that make a piece of music unique to us. That is the interpretation of the composer or songwriter. Much can be learned from knowing who wrote the music. Was that person a pianist writing for other instruments or a musician of any type composing to include piano, harp, or electronics?

For example, many times composers that are adept at using the computer will step the notes and rhythm into their computer very slowly and then speed it up to the tempo they like. Many times, that makes it impossible for an instrumentalist to play their music at the tempo they are hearing. So, we may have to leave out some less important notes just to play the music. Or another example is a pianist writing for an orchestral instrument. Do they know how to phrase their music for a flute or violin, and do they consider or understand what exactly an orchestral instrument can do?

In Chapter 8 of Part I, I had a quote from András Schiff that said, "a bar line is like a jail cell." I see phrasing all the time where the musical line goes over the bar line, but the phrasing mark is kept within the bar line. This is exactly the time to use our knowledge to place the phrasing line above the notes that are married together.

THE BUSINESS OF MUSIC

So, if you have done all of this for 20 years or so, and you are more than just a good musician, you should be ready to learn the "business" of music.

Consider if you are a soloist, a chamber music group, a jazz band, or any saleable entity. Why should you have an agent, a publicist, recordings, social media involvement, and other help? Then there is your package with still photos and a video. Oh, and don't forget to keep practicing every day.

The reason is someone else can always sell you better than you can sell yourself. It's easy for someone to say how great you are and why you should be hired. It is much more difficult for you to say it yourself as it borders on narcissism.

If you can't afford all the help, or you are not "discovered," you will have to do it yourself. That takes a lot of time away from playing and practicing. The businessperson in your group should be spending a minimum of two hours a day just looking for opportunities for your group. Or if you are a soloist, you must do that yourself.

Just a warning: There are many agents out there who will ask you to give them money so they can do the work for you. It is so much better if they do the work for you and then take a percentage. That's called *a work incentive* instead of *an agent for hire*. There are also attorneys in the music and entertainment business that besides being able to make you a water-tight contract (employers seldom back out of paying you BTW), they can have some great contacts that can help you.

#36

Never Compare
Yourself to Others

When you compare yourself to others, you are looking to win something: To be smarter, more creative, better than, and be looked up to more than the next person. It is an act of our own injured ego. Others around you notice this even if it's not a conscious part of their thinking. In the short and long run, this will injure us, as the people who are better than you may have a bigger ego than you and want to crush you, and the person who is not as good as you will notice your contempt for them.

It's important to remember that people are doing the best that they can. Yes, they can be better if they didn't have the hurdles put in front of them by themselves, family, friends, and enemies. I seem to remember there is a saying about walking in someone else's shoes.

Wouldn't it be nice if we could all let our jealousies and egocentric thoughts go and help one another? This is a nice thought but not likely to happen.

So, we are left with improving ourselves and not looking down on someone that doesn't have our tools or drive. To do that we must see them as people and not as competitors, and whenever possible, help them as gently as we can. And while we are improving ourselves as musicians and human beings, we learn from those who have more tools than us. We can learn quite a lot by listening and not talking. And there is nothing wrong with asking an occasional question.

Comparing yourself to others keeps you busy thinking about interpersonal relationships, and not about music, practicing, and performing. It's a waste of your time to compare yourself to others.

Now, comparing yourself to the general standard of a group you might be performing with is different because it entices you to pull your own weight in rehearsals and performances.

But wait, it's important to remember that those other musicians may have a different interest in music than you. They may feel more or less a desire to work at the same level or higher than the ensemble.

The level of the ensemble and its members' desire to keep the standard becomes more important and obvious as we age, and the musicians with less interest will drop out.

Now let me contradict myself!

Jazz musicians like to have cut sessions during a jam session where they try and play better than everyone else. Then there are always the conventions for each instrument where the display hall sounds like everyone trying to play their best lick better than the other 200 people in the hall—all a byproduct of competitive learning.

The school band or orchestra director's way of keeping a standard is a competition, which makes improvement personal. Though not teaching the love of music, instead, this method does work for competitive students. It's the fastest way for a music director to improve an ensemble but not a very pleasant one for the members.

I know why it doesn't or wouldn't happen, but what if? What if in a band every member in the section had to play 1st for a week, 2nd for a week, and 3rd for a week? Would that be a wake-up call? Of course, most of the section would likely quit out of embarrassment. Is that good or bad? Is it worth a one-time trial? Well, it's just a thought.

All people are so completely different from one another that I think it's amazing. Just look closely at the people around you and you will understand what I am saying. Their looks, their thinking, and everything about them are radically different. Yet somehow when playing music, they must come together and play music. Some like the competitive approach and some shun it. There is not much you can do about it except lead by example. That is playing the best you can every time you take your instrument out.

Music is not like football, basketball, or any sport. Music is only a team effort when rehearsing or performing. Practice is a solitary action most of the time, as opposed to team sports where you practice daily with the people you perform with.

So how do you learn to practice alone when no one teaches you how to deal with your special solitary time? Are you practicing winning the first chair in your ensemble? Or are you using your solitary time to learn about yourself and train yourself in the discipline of music, while studying music as an art, and at the same time as you improve, your perspective is enhanced? You can teach yourself through introspection and experimentation to be better at your craft and art.

You are creating beauty and whether you learn that through competition or inspiration, always keep in your mind the beauty of silence and introspection along with learning your notes and concept.

A private instructor always helps your discipline (which is different from competition) in your practice/alone time. Bear in mind, your teacher is teaching you their concept, which is good and bad. The good is that almost all of us sound like someone else before we sound like ourselves. The bad thing is if you pick the wrong private teacher and don't realize it, you will have their concept. Of course, as we get older and leave our first teachers, we know more about what we are looking for and can pick our private teachers with more knowledge about who we want to be artistically.

When starting music at a young age, parents become very important in selecting a teacher and overseeing our practice. I can tell you from experience that some practice we enjoy and some we don't. But it's important to do what the private teacher is asking and your parents are hopefully monitoring.

The best thing about private teachers is they don't have a reason to make you practice for a competitive reason. They teach you music and art and leave the rest to providence.

Remember like others, you bring uniqueness to music, and always remember how important your unique playing is as a part of your success.

So, my last suggestion is that you learn to want to play better and practice better, without competition in mind, but with artistic beauty as the centerpiece of your time. We are all students and as my friend Manny reminded me today, we learn something every day. And some days we learn a lot. So, PAY ATTENTION!

After the Pandemic, What?

The simple answer is VIDEO.

There will always be a market for live music. However, more people are staying at home and watching and listening to it at home.

People want to see us play. Some go to concerts, some stay home, but most people listen mostly or partially with their eyes. They want to see us in the act of creation and doing something that most of the time is not edited or sidelined.

Just go to YouTube and look for your favorite musicians; they will likely be there. Or look up your favorite piece of music; it's probably there as well. Look up a teacher on your instrument or style of music and it's there.

I went to YouTube and entered Brahms and clarinet, and I stopped counting at 30 entries. And that's just one example. There are some more challenging entries that may have only one video file. However, I think you get the idea. And that's but one of many video sites that have music videos you can watch. These sites are so ubiquitous that I don't have any idea of how many are available.

With the idea of video editing, plenty of what you see is sidelined (the musicians pretend to play, along with their pre-recorded music). But by the same token, there are plenty of live performed, videotaped performances.

The videotaped performances are where you can tell, like the opening of the *Rite of Spring* by Stravinsky, where a musician might have to sweat a bit on their first note. Some people like that; the feeling of a Porsche going full bore down an icy mountain road. You can see the performer emote or react to the music as it is played.

In the commercial area, including television and motion pictures, many if not most of the composers are so adept at the synthesizer and its many sounds that they pretty much write the whole score and then send it via email to a few soloists who add their part to be sent back to the composer to create a more authentic feeling to the music. Will this be the future after the pandemic? We all hope not, but many composers have found that this is an easier way to create products and not have to deal with the personalities of 80 musicians in one room. Plus, they make way more money.

Perhaps you have seen a split-screen with one person playing multiple parts. This technique existed before the pandemic, but rapidly became a way for musicians to express themselves and get their musical message to the public. And that is even with the knowledge that they had to learn both audio recording and video recording, and the editing of both disciplines. Or hire someone to do it for them.

It seems this is a mandatory addition to be added to teaching music, theater, and even video art.

Schools have always been a few years behind in adding new subject matter to the curriculum, simply because the teachers and administrators are so busy with their jobs, they don't have time to experiment with new techniques. I will say that a few colleges have this type of study but not nearly enough. In addition, many young people are learning on their own with their adeptness on the computer from a very young age. So how early should these types of study begin?

Many of you with positions in the music performance arena will not have to deal with the idea of recording yourself with both audio and video. However, those musicians not ensconced with a position in a group of some kind or as a soloist will benefit from the new techniques for learning, performing, and educating.

I have found that despite the frustrations of starting at the beginning with strange new techniques to help myself, there is a big payoff to having the knowledge. As a musician for over 50 years, and feeling most comfortable on my instruments, the frustration is more about the time it takes to learn alien programs, than the intent of learning something new and making mistakes like a beginner again. It doesn't have to take the place of practicing but can enhance practicing just by taking a little time to add something new.

Give it some thought. Are you willing to take on a new challenge that will enhance your music (you will listen and see differently), or do you want to stay where you are, doing what you are doing, at the speed you are doing it?

I guarantee you that the extra hour or two it takes to add new skills is worth the enhancement to your understanding.

I learned, or should I say am learning, from private teachers, as at my age school seems a bit difficult, and private lessons give much more information in an hour than a school class can give simply by how many students need their questions answered.

I hope you will embrace this change that is bound to become more of the norm in the years to come.

And by the way, you can see my most recent videos on YouTube. This is an interview with Ken McCarthy and the *Jazz on the Tube Podcast* about my career.

https://www.youtube.com/watch?v=Jn6ZB0TfMLQ&t=670s

This is a homemade video that I filmed and edited, on Starting Music, which is for those thinking about starting a music study, young and older students, and teachers. Also included is the idea of the importance of piano as part of music study.

https://www.youtube.com/watch?v=ESZiLdIGEj8&t=4s

#38

Leaving Music

We all leave music at some point. It may be the grim reaper has come to take us or an accident may take our abilities away. It could be a 4th grader who finds out that it is time-consuming and not a team sport.; that there is practicing (or perhaps a better word would be study) involved. Or computer games are more fun.

Let me start with the professional musician and move backward. I know many professional musicians who when their age is, let's say 65 years old, or as the business changes, they put the instrument down and retire. They may find another career, or if they have saved their money and invested wisely, might just have a couple of homes in beautiful places, and or travel the world until they must go into assisted living. Let's face it, the body does finally fail us all. It was just a way to make a living and they walked away content to move on in life.

Then there are those people like me who play for a living if we can and will continue to play until our body fails us. For me, music is my religion. For others, it is one of their religions or not a religion at all. At any rate, it is something we must continue to do. I am 76 at the time of this writing and fight certain frailties as I age, but I don't quit. I hope to finish a jazz album and a classical album by the end of the year, and I am finishing writing this book about music and life. I also continue to write these blogs, although I'm having a tougher time finding new ideas to discuss. So, if you know of something that I have missed of importance, please tell me.

Then there are music teachers, the angels in our lives, that get to the point of deciding whether to continue teaching or not. Or they may be told by their contract or the schools they work for it's time to retire. They too may be leaving because they must or it's their choice to enjoy the golden years. We all know there are many jokes about the golden years.

Many musicians in high-stress jobs, like playing a principal chair in a great symphony orchestra, just can't take the heat of preparing new music constantly and visiting the war-horse pieces the audience loves so much. They too know when it's time. Their relationship with music may continue or they may just decide to relax. We all know the commitment to the art and craft of music is a long arduous journey. And there are always the young players that keep getting better every generation knocking on every door.

There are well-trained musicians in colleges and conservatories who realize that commitment is not what they really want to continue. Many times, these people who have come so far will find a music-related field, and there are many that they are more comfortable with. Some will give up music altogether and only keep an appreciation of the arts. That is important too. Others will find another specialty that they either enjoy or that pays an immense amount of money.

Younger students may find out it's just not what they had envisioned or are interested in doing. Then there are the very young students that are doing it because their parents thought it would keep them off the streets along with karate, etc. Or perhaps they just wanted to introduce them to music and the arts. Then there is the brave young person that just thinks they might enjoy playing music and then after a while just decides it's not for them.

Then there is the big decider: The music business changes.

No matter what genre we have decided to pursue, the business will change. Classical music usually changes the slowest, but it still changes. Pop music is the most volatile, as every generation has its own music that was developed in a garage somewhere and becomes the accompaniment for the story of their life.

For whatever reason we leave music and whenever we leave music, it's my hope that our time will be remembered fondly. I have a physical trainer who said he played the flute for 6 years when he was young. He said it was a great experience. He smiled when he said it. That is what I hope for all of us. A smile and a love of music.

PART THREE

A Broader Look at Life's Problems

These are musings that have come to mind, as no matter what you do for a living, these subjects affect your life. Of course, they are of a very American perspective as the United States is where I have spent most of my life. Readers from other parts of the world will find something in these writings too. And the best thing is you don't have to agree with anything I have written. These subjects are just to give you something to think about. So, take a moment after reading each subject and think about it for a minute or two.

Politics

Charley Reese was a columnist for the *Orlando Sentinel* for 49 years and what is presented here is his last column before retiring, originally published on February 3, 1984. This is about as clear and easy to understand as it can be. It is his view of the American Political System but can certainly be used to share or contrast his views in other countries. The article is politically neutral and does not represent the left, right, or centrist way of thinking. This article is worth remembering.

525 VS. 300,000,000

545 people are responsible for the mess,
but they unite in a common con

By Charley Reese

Politicians are the only people in the world who create problems and then campaign against them.

Have you ever wondered why, if both Democrats and the Republicans are against deficits, we have deficits? Have you ever wondered why, if all the politicians are against inflation and high taxes, we inflation and high taxes?

You and I don't propose the federal budget. The President does. You and I don't have the constitutional authority to vote on appropriations. The House of Representatives does.

You and I don't write the tax code. The Congress does. You and I don't set fiscal policy, the Congress does. You and I don't control the monetary policy, The Federal Reserve Bank does.

One hundred senators, 435 congressmen, one president, and nine Supreme Court justices—545 human beings out of 238 million—are directly, legally, morally and individually responsible for the domestic problems the plague this county.

I excluded the members of the Federal Reserve Bank because that problem was created by the Congress. In 1913, Congress delegated its constitutional duty to provide a sound currency to a federally chartered but private central bank.

I excluded all the special interest and lobbyists for a sound reason. They have no legal authority. They have no ability to coerce a senator, a congressman or a president to do one cotton-picking thing. I don't care if they offer a politician $1 million in cash. The politician has the power to accept or reject it.

No matter what the lobbyist promises, it's the legislator's responsibility to determine how he votes.

Don't you see now the con game that is played on the people by the politicians? Those 545 human beings spend much of their energy convincing you that what they did is not their fault. They cooperate in this common con regardless of party.

What separates a politician from a normal human being is an excessive amount of gall. No normal human being would have the gall of a speaker, who stood up and criticized the president for creating deficits.

The president can only propose a budget. He cannot force the Congress to accept it. The Constitution, which is the supreme law of the land, gives sole responsibility to the House of Representatives for originating appropriations and taxes. O'Neill is speaker of the House. He is the leader of the majority party. He and his fellow Democrats, not the president, can approve any budget they want. If the president vetoes it, they can pass it over his veto.

Just 545 Americans have fouled up this great nation.

It seems inconceivable to me that a nation of 300 million cannot replace 545 people who stand convicted—by present facts—of incompetence and irresponsibility. I can't think of a single domestic problem, from an unfair tax code to defense overruns, that is not traceable directly to those 545 people.

When you fully grasp the plain truth that 545 people exercise the power of the federal government, then it must follow that what exists is what they want to exist.

If the tax code is unfair, it's because they want it unfair. If the budget is in the red, it's because they want it in the red. If the Marines are in Lebanon, it's because they want them in Lebanon.

There are no insoluble government problems. Do not let these 545 people shift the blame to bureaucrats, whom they hire and whose jobs they can abolish; to lobbyists, whose gifts and advice they can reject; to regulators, to whom they give the power to regulate and from whom they can take it.

Above all, do not let them con you into the belief that there exist disembodied mystical forces like "the economy," "inflation," or "politics" that prevent them from doing what they take an oath to do.

These 545 people, and they alone, are responsible. They and they alone, have the power. They, and they alone, should be held accountable by the people who are their bosses—provided that they have the gumption to manage their own employees.

Politics is the Entertainment Division
of the Military Industrial Complex.
—**Frank Zappa**

I have learned that to ignore the facts
doesn't change the facts.
—**Andy Rooney**

The more corrupt the state the more numerous the laws.
—**Tacitus, 56-120 AD,**
The Annals of Imperial Rome

War

What a sad commentary on these animals we know as human beings.

I had a history teacher in high school that said, "History is the story of real estate changing hands."

Is it that simple, and/or are we that greedy? It seems we are that greedy. Of course, there is always internal strife in many countries and that leads to civil war. We all say we don't want war. So, why is there war between countries and internally within a country.

Is this just the way that the animal with the most brainpower acts? It seems so. Though there are many wonderful people, there are many really wounded people who seem to need whatever attention and power they can muster even if it's illegal, and even if it leads to war.

The United States has been at war since the end of WWII. Many other countries cling to internal or external war. In general, that is the action of a country with leaders that want control other countries and the people and resources controlled by those countries.

Our mantra seems to be "whatever is in our national interest," and it's the mantra of many countries, thus many governments, thus the people that control the destiny of those countries. These leaders seem to think because they have power, they have the respect of the citizens. That is to be debated. Especially when the government is dysfunctional. I find it interesting that the children of politicians seldom go to war. They stay home, protected. The politicians think their family is above getting in the trenches.

Make no mistake—with all our worldwide weaponry, tanks, missiles, drones, supersonic jets, and about every weapon you can think of—we don't even know how to take war out of the trenches, war is still fought in the trenches. Trenches are not nice places. Our warriors are living and sleeping in dirt, hiding behind trees, lying flat in the marshes, eating out of a can, dealing with rain, heat, humidity, and being mostly miserable, all of which changes their life forever.

Internal wars seem to be about the needs of the poorer and poorest people versus the elite, rich people who mostly control the government... and have the good weapons. These weapons are mostly purchased from another country and possibly a country they will be at war with in the future. Or we sell the weapons to our friends and enemies, so the military industrial economy stays healthy. Of course, we keep the best weapons for ourselves that even our citizens know nothing about.

Most animals kill to eat and only to eat, or protect themselves from some other animal trying to eat them. NOT HUMANS though. We kill and criminals kill for power, prestige, and expansion of their control of our world. Just like a country, a criminal kills, because they think they must protect themselves. They don't see themselves as bad people, just someone that is living a tough life and needs to take care of themselves by devious means.

War is terrible, perhaps the most terrible thing used by humankind. Is this really who we are? It seems so.

Despite all the great music, art, dance, literature and all the positive skills we possess, we seem to gravitate wanting power and living better than someone else. I am not saying there are not good people with the highest ideals. I am saying that is not how life seems to be lived. And lived from almost the beginning of time.

Is that humanity? Or is that how humanity does its work? Either way, it's a terrible way to live.

Culture

There is more than one type of culture and one kind of art. It seems the two main categories would be pop culture and classical culture, or native culture, whether local or worldwide. There is also ethnic culture, and many more, perhaps even including your culture or your relationship with world culture.

I can say that my culture is musical, having performed throughout my school days, and professionally in classical, jazz, pop, and celebrity accompaniment, opera, musical theater (Broadway musicals), symphonic music, chamber music, big band jazz, small group jazz, and having recorded 9 CDs of my own in different genres. Etc.

But that is only one type of culture in the mixed bag we must consider in being truly "cultured."

What about painting, sculpture, pottery, dance, music, literature, and the other forms of culture that have been with us since the beginning of humankind? Now we have pop and classical culture that includes audio recordings, television, video recordings, comic books, mixed media, and many more cultural activities that we can all collectively add to this list.

For those who live in the United States, it's easier to learn about our own culture first. Read books by American authors. There are many classics both older and newer. An old one could be *Huckleberry Finn*. A new one could be a novel by Dan Brown, Jody Picoult, Maya

Angelou, or some other contemporary writer. Look at American art—at a museum or from a book. Listen to American composers, Leonard Bernstein and Ned Rorem are examples. Then there is American popular music. I call it popular music, composers light, or troubadours. These are easier to understand for the novice and there is nothing at all wrong with that. In fact, with pop art or so-called serious art, you will find music that you like and music you don't like. Make sure to try and figure out what it is you like about each genre.

In the long run, I don't think there is much that is "bad" music. Music at its very least keeps its practitioners busy and out of "trouble."

If you really listen to or study music and art that you don't understand, you may change your mind about the subject you are studying. What we don't want to do is only accept the art that we like simply because that's what we grew up with. The whole idea of art, besides its intrinsic beauty, is that as we study it more we see more, and we grow more. Very few readers have started with Shakespeare with a complete understanding of the language. That type of high art is something to grow into.

I remember when I first played Brahms, I didn't get it because I wasn't ready for it yet. The notes were not that hard to play so I thought it wasn't so great. But as I grew as a musician knowing where to place those notes to make the music understandable to an audience made me grow. So, at the ripe early age of 50, I started to understand Brahms. Now 25 years later I think I almost own it.

The thing about high art and culture—we grow into it. Pop culture is something we live in as an accompaniment to our lives. But that accompaniment to our lives could be high art if we took a little time every day to improve ourselves, through listening, looking, studying, reading, and in general being open to everything that is not a part of our prejudice at this moment.

Computers

THE GOOD AND THE BAD

Let me start with my personal feelings about computers. About half the time I would like to take a hammer and smash it as my blood pressure hits 200. The rest of the time I like it and find it helpful. That's just an opinion. My opinion.

There are many situations in life that are both good and bad for us and for the world as well. The computer can be such a helpful device for all we do—and it can be the reason for such terror in our lives.

I would say that if one were to pay attention and have a little computer education, they would see us utilizing the computer or computer chips every few minutes. Most of us carry around a cellular phone, better called a cellular computer, that will do everything a laptop computer can do.

THE GOOD

There are so many great things about a computer. Once mastered, which you already know I have not done, there are so many positive things about computers that I can only touch on some of them. By the same token, those of you born a few years later than me will find the computer to be just another tool in your life box of tools. And we all share many things computers do for us that we don't think about. Like starting your car, for example.

We have office programs with spreadsheets, word apps, mail programs, graphic programs, and more. We have programs that let us hold a meeting for lots of people or just two. There are programs to remember our passwords for us since every website either needs to be found or logged into. We have music programs with literally millions of selections either for listening or purchase. We have video programs that have music, video, instructions for fixing our own computer, or adding new programs. We can make CDs and burn them to disk plus many other functions. There are programs that let us send huge files to one or more people.

There are accounting programs, games, and Internet connection to every website that is available. We can edit our own pictures, or make a movie, or a music file (in the old days called CDs).

Access to the Internet opens whole new worlds to follow and it is our choice on which ones interest us. We get to meet lots of people on social media and meet people in our Internet travels.

We can speed up or slow down music and have the pitch stay the same. Or we can change the pitch to fit a new project or practice routine. There are so many music lessons on the computer, especially jazz instruction that are available to all of us. I would like to remind you, however, that you also need a private teacher and not depend totally on the Internet.

In general, the computer has raised the intellect of people with the information they can obtain so quickly. When I was in high school, nobody typed except those taking business or secretarial classes. Now almost everyone types. So that's just one example of how the computer has improved our capabilities.

Our computers control machinery, do repetitive work that we don't want to do; they create the bills we get (yuk!) and the invoices we send (yay!). Computers help run our cars, elevators, phones, timers, and about 80% of everything we do.

Where do I stop? These are just some of the things that are possible. Just go to the store for either the PC or the Mac and start looking at the many programs made for you. Or type in anything you are looking for in your browser and see what's available. Those sources are available for anyone that wants to see them (although there are thousands of programs you will never be allowed to see, sometimes called the dark web). So, that's just a smidgeon of the positive things about the computer.

And probably the big thing for us is that computers can be used to compose and arrange music—many times by just one person. It's good for the programmer, but not so good for the future of live music. Especially commercial music.

THE BAD

Boom! Most world weaponry is controlled by computers: ICBM, Inter Continental Ballistic Missiles. That's the big one, a missile fired from one country and the way we have them situated, can be delivered to any other country, and hit a target the size of an average front lawn or smaller. Missiles are delivered from the air, and missiles are delivered by airplane too. And, of course, ocean naval weapons are also controlled by computers. Computers are now used for land forces in many ways too. It's the new way of war. It seems we always need ground forces to clean up our messes and they know where they are within inches with the equipment they carry.

There is a command center several places in the world that can control a large drone carrying varying sized warheads and delivered into the window of a building. The command center watches everything the drone does in real time.

How about the dark web. A computer can take down any electrical grid, control water distribution, and even drive your personal computer to take us to the nut house by losing use of it when we need it the most.

There is an argument on how accurate computers are in counting votes. I think they are pretty accurate in counting votes; however it creates a chance for us to see the worse in people that don't agree with the outcome of an election.

Computers have cut in half the number of working musicians; again, affecting commercial music more than classical music.

Computers run our houses, our cars, and every moving thing you can think of, and it will just keep becoming more ubiquitous.

Marriage

As you will read, I am speaking of a classic model of marriage. I dare not go into alternative thoughts on marriage and relationships, as I am not an expert in such living styles.

In a classic marriage, women need to have a man that can help finance a family if it comes to happen. She needs to be reminded how important her life is and how much you appreciate her difficult work on behalf of you and the family. If you don't think it's difficult, all men should cook and wash the dishes three times a day, vacuum and dust the house, and do a few loads of washing. Water the lawn and clean the driveway and sidewalks and take care of their spouse and their children. And in the modern traditional marriage, add the possibility of going to work several days a week.

In a classic marriage, a man has testosterone. He spends his life learning how to mitigate his urges.

One thing is for sure. Life over the years will change many times in a relationship. So, both partners need to know how to calmly state their needs and change a bit with the outcome of the conversation. Don't argue, it shows disrespect and never fixes the many problems and adjustments necessary in a marriage. Besides arguing is seldom about the real problem.

We all hold deep secrets. Even the best of us.

It's good to talk about our secrets with our spouse if they are up to it. However, everyone has very deep secrets that are too painful or personal to share. Psychologists spend a lot of time and a lot of our money trying to get these secrets out of us so we can be happier people.

Most people will get married in their lifetime. Some will marry several times. It initially occurred to me that the only reason to get married was to have children. Upon re-examining my thinking, there are other reasons for matrimony: companionship, business partnerships, financial advantages, and other advantages that I am sure I have not thought of.

Having a child is the biggest risk you can take.

The primary reason though seems to be procreation. I have discussed many times so far; the importance and guidance offered to the child and the needs of the parents who must love a child as well as a spouse. As you can tell I am speaking about the needs of the parents. Once the parents have fulfilled the child's needs, it's important to take the time to take care of the needs of the parents. Repeat the things that brought you together. And do new things.

Of course, it's important to have some discipline to teach the child the essence of the local, state, or national traditions, both in being law-abiding and respectful of others. The other issue is how these things are taught to the young person. Is it corporal punishment or is it verbal lessons with an occasional recap of what the youngster has done to someone else and why that action is not acceptable? Teaching a child without injuring them is something to work on.

How many secrets does a youngster and even those in their teens carry with them? Like parents and adults, younger people harbor secrets. It's best in my opinion to minimize these secrets as the secret can waste much brainpower in going over and over it in one's own head.

In my own life, corporal punishment was never applied, *except once*. I told my dad a lie and he basically went berserk. I learned my lesson and saw the wisdom of never lying. Some people don't deserve the truth, so that must be considered, but it's so much easier to never lie, as again this wastes brain power. My relationship with my family became so much better as we could speak the truth without any worry about the outcome just because we didn't agree with each other. The no lie filtered into the rest of my life and made it better. And frankly, being a musician is all about truth.

Love at first sight. Does that promise a great marriage? No, it only guarantees love at first sight. Do people love each other equally? I would say, very seldom. Do two people have the same sexual appetite? It's very helpful. Do couples see each other in an accepting way (pheromones)? Over the years couples change how they look and think, in addition to becoming different people from reacting to a spouse and a changing and aging world.

It's important for two people considering marriage to spend a lot of time together before marriage even to the point of living together. A peaceful spouse and an explosive spouse will have many difficulties in marriage. Living together for a year or more (2 to 10 years) helps with these kinds of differences that can ruin a marriage. You may even find cohabitation more beneficial.

Love is certainly a part of marriage, but so is friendship and communication. If marriage is only about love or one partner being lonely, or so many other things that enter a marriage, a marriage union is bound to fail. Failed marriages are very expensive from giving up things such as a house or money that is shared, or most important, if there are children, the toll it will take on them. No matter what is decided about the disposition of children, they are bound to be injured. There is also pain for everyone in the marriage as it splits and usually lasts for many years later.

Marriage is also about personalities. If one of the partners is a jokester and the other partner finds no happiness in the jokes, it makes it very difficult to communicate. Or is that all that it is about? Communication? I think more.

I think the most important thing in any relationship, including marriage, is for both people to have the best interests of the other person as a primary goal. That also goes for your offspring. Your children should know you have their best interests at heart and are not trying to infringe into their life. Supporting everyone in your family assures a happy relationship.

Almost immediately after writing this I attended a 60th wedding anniversary and asked the couple what the secret of 60 years of a relatively happy marriage was. They both agreed—having time to themselves for whatever they wanted to do whenever they wanted to do it.

I feel I must include a paragraph on sex in marriage, though I am sure it will infuriate some people (can't we talk about everything?). Sex is almost always important in a marriage, especially in younger people, and if it doesn't exist, marriage is not a viable relationship. As we get older, getting married without the idea of a strong sexual relationship can be generally accepted. There may be still some of that dangerous testosterone lingering in males though. What do you ladies that have gone through the change of life think of that and how are you going to handle this dilemma?

Some people believe that sex should not be consummated unless it's after marriage. My humble opinion is this idea could not be more incorrect. It is my opinion that a long period of sexual adjustment is important. Frequency, technique, equality of expectations, and thoughts of sexual intensity are all important. To get married and have the first conjugal experience on the wedding night might sound romantic, but is usually a recipe for disaster, as the couple will have to unwind for many years, or until a sexual agreement can be mutually agreed upon or the marriage fails at some sooner or later time.

Concept is a large part of sex. If it were just as easy as all sex is the same, it would be easy. However, think of everyone you know. They all look different, they all talk a little differently, they all think about things differently, and they all have a different libido. You may see a group of women or a group of men talking about sex, but you will rarely see a group of men and women at the same time discussing the subject seriously and calmly. There would be too many hurt feelings and too many strained relationships because of sharing such a taboo subject. Even in the "sexual generation" this holds true. I don't think we can have a good marriage without good sex. Regularity may be up for discussion, but the quality must be one that both spouses agree upon.

Of course, children and aging change the regularity of conjugal matters, and partners figure out that it is as much about having the other person's best interests at heart—all the time. Yet, sex, until a couple is very aged, is always looming in the background somewhere. I am old enough to say that but not old enough to forget about it.

One good way to find out what you may have in store for you in marriage is to look at the marriage of your partner's parents. It is said, "the apple doesn't fall far from the tree." Your partner learned a lot from their parents, and unless they paid close attention to their own feelings and understanding, they are likely to be much like their parents in many ways.

It takes a good period of a lifetime to realize that the friendship form of love is as important as the carnal pleasures of love. The best we can hope for is that everyone is able to experience that much earlier than later. And have both. Or you could go to a psychologist or read a lot of books on the subject. You can check the Internet.

Oh, just one more thing. People can love multiple people. The purpose of marriage is a partnership that lets the other partner love without violating the sanctity of the marriage. There are many loveable people in the world and thus confusion. Many people think that if their spouse loves other people, it diminishes the marriage. I am not talking about having sex with every person you love. Sometimes that other person you love can improve your marriage. Your spouse must understand they are the partner you chose and that you will always protect them.

If a person gets married and then divorces, or marries and divorces several times, are we learning a lesson from the marriage(s)? It may not be immediate given the initial pain, but hopefully each of us can use a divorce to improve ourselves and help understand what we are really looking for in a marriage.

We have all been injured in our relationships. How well do we forgive and move on or do we harbor that pain forever as one of our dark secrets and the opportunity to be bitter.

Well again, one more thought. Don't get married because you are lonely. You may just find out that once in a marriage you are still lonely. A dilemma for sure.

And once again I will suggest to you in times of stress, try singing your complaint. It's very difficult to sing and argue at the same time.

Honor

The dictionary lists one of the meanings of the word honor to be "adherence to what is right or to a conventional standard of conduct." Here is an example:

"I must, as a matter of honor, avoid any taint of dishonesty."

I was going to write a longer piece on honor, however, the dictionary hits it right on the head.

There are different types of honor we learn during our life: There is the honor we learn from our parents (well, perhaps not all get that information); the honor we learn in the military, especially in one of the officer's programs or academies; the honor we learn in our profession; and the honor we learn with our friends.

So, given that we accept the dictionary definition of avoiding any taint of dishonesty with honor also being truth we must consider a few things.

Who deserves our honor—and if they don't, how do we handle the situation? We must be truthful and honest, yet be careful not to hurt someone. So, there are times when we must sidestep any situation that may become violent—verbally or physically—hurtful to another person or ourselves. We can and should deflect those who would attack us without honor. In the words of the author Tom Clancy "Honor is a man's gift to himself."

> *Honor is a man's gift to himself.*
> **—Tom Clancy**

Taking Chances

Chances are experiments that teach us.

If we are not willing to take a chance to learn something new, we become reclusive and inflexible in learning. Jack Wheaton, one of my college professors, used to say learning is a painful process. The same can be true of taking chances. In both cases, it is important to take calculated chances or risks. Did I say calculated? That's the only way not to hurt ourselves. But then again, I think we have all taken chances that weren't calculated, or sometimes never planned, as a situation can force us into it. Like the student that must give a correct answer and just guesses.

The skier stands at the top of a high jagged mountaintop and jumps to the snow for an exciting and dangerous ride down a steep slope. That's taking a chance and the skier most likely knows there is a risk they could get hurt, but they prepare with training and proper equipment. That is a calculated risk, and yes, taking a chance.

The first time a student goes on stage to play a recital piece, they are also taking a chance, as they have never experienced walking out in front of an audience before. That is a risk because they don't know the outcome. But no matter how the outing turns out, good or bad, it's an education.

So, in the two scenarios I have described, there was a dangerous chance and a safer chance. While both are dangerous in nature, in one scenario there is a chance of a physical disaster, even becoming a paraplegic, and in the other a mental disaster. However, in each scenario, the participant learns something. So, chances can almost always be a learning experience. The trick, of course, is taking a chance where we learn something without injuring ourselves in any way.

Then there are stupid risks that people take that can affect others. Like riding past another car on the right on the fringe of a road at 70 mph. The driver on the right knows in the back of their mind that they are making a stupid move. Or another example would be driving 50 mph in front of a school while it's in session.

So that lets us know that there are good chances and bad chances to be taken. In general, I would say the chance should be thought out before we take it, although chances are made by our subconscious occasionally too.

Everything that's not in our routine becomes a chance. That is how we learn. But better yet, we can learn from someone else who has also taken a chance and see the outcome of that endeavor. In either instance, we are learning from a chance taken.

Different personalities will tolerate different types of chance. Aggressive people and timid people still learn from their own chances and the chances of others.

So, I say don't be afraid of taking a calculated chance and enjoy the personal growth that comes with it.

Original Thinking

Original thinking is a difficult thing to cultivate. Or should I say *non-thinking*? We are constantly being bombarded with other people's thinking—advertisements, television and streaming shows, books, websites, social media, friends, enemies, society, family, religion, penal law, magazines, and I could go on. Where does someone else's thinking stop in trying to puncture your cells with their beliefs? It starts with you making your cell walls thicker and not allowing diseased thinking to enter your being.

How do we clear our cluttered mind of everything and start with an empty mind—a mind that leaves faulty thoughts by the wayside? That really is the only way of accepting what we really think, see, or believe, as opposed to what we are told to think, see, or believe.

The best place for original thinking is when alone and in a quiet environment—practicing music, painting, original writing, or any other activity that is not a group activity. As proof of this idea, find a piece of music you like, get as many recordings and live performances as you can find. You will notice one thing if you have educated ears. Every performance is different. That is *original thinking*. It is also self-education.

Many times, what you hear may be at the insistence of a teacher, but as the performer becomes older and wiser, the original thinking becomes clearer.

I had a friend who was a brilliant pianist. When he would comment on something, it always sounded obtuse and completely original. He saw things differently. Originality. Like his piano playing.

I think part of this idea is just how you are brought up in the family environment. And part of it is realizing that almost everything we see on any media of any type is affecting us. We are being inundated with a strong belief or a strong wish for the consumer. It's also done with very expensive images to help build the view of those that would control us.

Especially in video presentations, the presenters have control of every pixel and where every image came from. Even a green screen is taking over more and more of our beliefs by creating any background or foreground and fooling us to believe in a visual fantasy. With three or more camera shots of any single thing, we are able to see things we would never see live. Kind of cool . . . yet kind of deceptive.

Another way of thinking about clear thinking is to look at the gurus in East India. They spend a lifetime working on the idea of no thought, even to the point of living in caves for years to avoid stimulation. Even these gurus say they can't maintain this level of non-thinking for long amounts of time and that thinking in a normal world has its place.

At any rate, become original. Find new ways to describe what you see and new ways to perform your new insights. Gain insight with your new originality. Be original.

The Business Triangle

I keep talking about business and saying you should save your money. Here is another idea that has been around for a long time—and many people use it in selecting a vendor (musician amongst other things) or as an idea to live by.

A triangle, of course, consists of 3 sides. A *business triangle* consists of:

Speed—How fast will it get done?

Cost—How much is the finished price?

Quality—How good is the quality of workmanship?

The most common answer is to be told to pick two of the three options. If you offer all three you are likely to get more jobs. These are general rules most businesses such as construction, computer repair, and business in general fall into. Most people have had the experience of only getting two of the three sides of the triangle. It's true in many industries.

It's not true in music, where a musician or an ensemble is providing the service. The musician is required to be on time, do a good job, and be affordable. As I believe all things should be. Of course, this is not true of the top 10% of performers who can ask for more money. However, they are still expected to provide all three elements of the triangle.

Most musicians don't know what they charge and unless the pay is extremely poor, the musician(s) are likely to take whatever is offered. It's the job of the musician to know what other musicians of the same ilk are charging and to maintain the whole triangle.

Or is it?

Musicians, in general, should know what they are worth and in a perfect world hold out for that price. Many times a union or some other entity will negotiate for the musician and may charge the employers a different price for the same services. Businesspeople know what things cost from the business triangle and will usually pick the lowest price, be it from an individual or a group of musicians.

Then there is supply and demand. The market is supply oriented in these days of the early 21st century as there are so many good, and even fantastic, musicians available, that unless musicians and those that represent us are immovable in the cost, wages will wane to an embarrassing low level.

One of the problems is we have not told the public or many of our employers what we are worth and why. Also, there are always musicians willing to work for less just to get the job.

Don't Worry, Be Happy

TIP 1

I have been teaching for almost as long as my professional music career—somewhere around 50 years (although I've never kept track of exactly when things happened in my life). In those 50 or so years my teaching has improved, of course, along with my insights into students and concepts. My students have ranged in age from between 10 and 85 years old.

Some students just like music and want to play in a school or community band. Others want to be professional musicians or professional teachers. In general, most have the same issues to be dealt with, even though they may have different psychological approaches to playing an instrument.

Although there is a big difference between what talent a student possesses and what mechanical skills they bring to the table, there seems to be a certain common dilemma that all students have, and that is the internal dialogue or thinking they bring with them to the lessons.

Almost all students and professionals experience negative emotions to one extent or another. That includes the novice student, the experienced student, and many professionals, including myself.

At times we simply think we are not good enough. We may be in the top 10 percent of our craft or even a world-famous soloist, and yet we sometimes question ourselves and allow negative emotions and thoughts to surface, which affects our brain chemistry and performance.

So…if we can harness our negative thoughts, we can improve our performance. We must concentrate on our thinking process and allow what comes from that to improve our performance. The more we can master our emotions as we improve our mechanics, the better we sound, and the more fun music becomes.

Seems simple, doesn't it? It's actually that simple.

When we practice or perform, we are concerned with the outcome of our hard work and repeated practice. We can continue to worry about the outcome of our practice and concertizing, or we can move our focus to the process of what we are doing and let the outcome of our practice and concerts act only as feedback to our efforts. This feedback, which is the result of our practice and concertizing, can feed our understanding of paying more attention to the process. In short, forget the results.

It seems to me that the feedback we get from playing should be applied to how we prepare. If we can concentrate on the preparation, the results are bound to improve. If we spend our waking hours worried about results and forget the process by which we practice and play, we are bound to stagnation. Our chance of improvement is diminished.

The next time you practice or play a concert, stop looking at how successful you are. Instead, play each phrase thinking only about the phrase and each note as it relates to the other notes. You will naturally hear the difference in your performance.

Another Bit of Advice

TIP 2

Fear cannot exist in the present. My friend Jack Reidling used to say, "No matter what you think it is going to be, it is going to be something different."

Try this: Stop reading for a moment. Close your eyes and open them back up quickly. What was happening at that exact moment? You were not thinking about the past or the future. You were in the moment. No fear of the future or regrets about the past. That's what is meant by "being in the present." It's not the past and not the future. In 99.99999 percent of the cases, when you closed and opened your eyes you were not thinking about the past or the future.

Fear of the future is not your friend—and the past can't be changed. Where we want to be is in the NOW.

You can't separate your mind and your body. Your mind controls your body. Your body doesn't have the power to control your mind. Emotion or fear causes your performance to diminish. Your performance can only be at its maximum ability when you are playing and *in the present*. That's when you are playing on instinct, through training.

Fear is about the future, and you aren't doing the future. You are doing the *now*. If you are practicing and fear the performance you have coming up, your performance will be diminished. That is guaranteed.

So simply don't worry about the performance. Don't worry about what you did in the past and just work on the technique of notes, phrasing, intonation, and all the other things that are part of music.

The result of not worrying or being in fear is relaxation. It's great to feel relaxed, but you may have to practice being in the moment to be relaxed, concentrating on what you are doing. Let the other thoughts pass through you and don't give them a second thought. Concentrating on the mechanics of what you do is the key to ridding yourself of thoughts that confuse your brain. You will find that your performance will feel like your practice—a desirable trait for sure.

How well you control the present determines your future outcome. Good or bad. Let's face it, we only have control of the present.

In previous chapters, I have talked about Zen—and that is simply what we are talking about here, the Zen of music. Zen is not that if you perform well, you will have enough power to do more concerts so you can buy a car, a house, or take a loved one to dinner. Ignoring the outcome is not for sissies. You must work on it to learn it. Have you spent your life worried about where you will be tomorrow, or in a month, a year, or ten years? All folly it seems. You and I cannot control the future. We can only control what we do each moment.

So, practice being in the moment every time you play a note, start a phrase, practice, or perform. Think about your notes and not your success. That is the best chance of ensuring your future no matter what that may be.

Music is not a life-or-death situation no matter how much you want it. Be patient, stay in the moment and the future will come. With less fear, you will play better.

Religion

This subject should be discussed by someone much braver than I. However, from what I have seen, experienced, and studied I will say this as my belief since none of us really know the facts.

Finding Jesus is what most people say. But what I think is that Jesus is a metaphor for recognizing one's birth and death, and the importance of one's frailties while alive.

Some people say religion is a monument for the things we don't understand, but I can't remember who said it.

Internal Dialogue

Internal dialogue is simply talking to yourself internally.

The great thing about music at an advanced level is there is little or no internal dialogue while performing.

Or conversely, the music is so under the performer's fingers that they can daydream or think about anything they want. This is not common, nor suggested.

One's internal dialogue is very important because if you are telling yourself the wrong things, it's detrimental to you. If you are telling yourself the right things, your life can be fabulous. Part of this study is watching people that are happy.

When a beginner learns to read a note, they first must see the note, then they must think of the name of the note, then the fingering of the note, and finally play the note. That's four things that must be done to play a note. Also included is holding the instrument and trying to get a good sound. At a certain point, they look at the note and the fingers can go where they are supposed to go by just seeing the note.

In general, talking to yourself while playing might mean you are not paying enough attention to the music. When you first start a piece, talking to yourself is understandable as you are trying to figure out how to play what's in front of you. After you learn the piece, your internal dialogue will stay around as you are not sure that you know a piece of music as well as it can be played. Once you own the piece of music, internal dialogue should be minimal or non-existent.

This idea of not talking to yourself started many centuries ago with the East Indians who would lock themselves in a cave and meditate all day and all night. It must be said though that even these gurus or sages don't achieve pure clarity of mind all the time. However, they do reach that level so often that even when they are not in what they call *Nirvana*, the non-internal dialogue spills over into their normal life.

So, if your internal dialogue can be trained to think happy thoughts, you will become happy even when bad things happen to you.

Artificial Intelligence

AI (artificial intelligence) now has become part of the current and future landscape. It can be noted, however, that the inventor of AI quit his job and now has serious misgivings about what AI will have for the future.

Here is a little story about what I was told 20 years ago: A good friend of mine, an excellent composer and pianist, had a sideline doing video production for weddings. The computer editing program he used for the video had a music function attached to it.

Mark told me that he had videotaped a wedding and was editing it along with the help of the happy couple. After editing the video of the wedding, he selected a bossa nova kind of piece for background music that the couple liked a lot.

The first thing to note, he did not write the music for the video; and being a composer it was something he could easily have done. But the couple loved the music they selected. A week or so later the couple came back and wanted to eliminate some of the video portion, which he did for them. Within a few seconds, the program composed an updated version of the music to fit the new length of the video. Without the program, it would have taken my friend a few hours to adjust the music for the shorter video.

I remind you that this was 20 years ago.

The couple loved the computer-programmed music, and my friend knew it was not worth his time to create a more beautiful score than the computer was capable of at the get-go. Sad commentary.

Now 20 years later we have AI that can write a motion picture and score the motion picture. Since the computer is internal, all the real live people are put out of business. The writers, the actors, the lighting people, even the caterers—literally everyone you see in the end credits of a motion picture. Thousands of jobs are potentially lost.

Then there is the music. The computer, using AI, can create a music score including all the live musicians it has collected music from, composing music with the sounds available that have been stolen—or worse paid for (those dumb musicians).

Even composers now that use a few musicians to make the score more believable are using orchestras as a source of their music. The Vienna strings, for example, can be purchased today as well as instruments and strings from many other famous orchestras. Soon these composers may be a thing of the past, as well as all the support people that help make music come to life.

If AI becomes available to many industries, who will pay people to sit at home and how will their value be based?

We can only hope that AI does not catch on or that laws can be enacted to protect workers, or it is going to be a very different world even in these days of fast changes on every platform. While it is immediately affecting the world of music and entertainment, every trade, craft, business, and executive should be on the lookout and fight to stop the unregulated use of this new technology.

My Final Words

If you want to be at the top of your chosen interest or business, you must study and know your material better than those around you. You must have the best teachers and your job must be your life. And remember to find an interest or job that you normally gravitate to so your job is in a way your hobby.

I play music. Music is my religion, my hobby, and one of the many loves of my life.

Be Happy

It's a choice you alone make.

PART FOUR

Quotes and Thoughts

Quotes are short, or sometimes long ideas we read or hear from someone else. It can even be the Horoscope in the daily newspaper. It can also be our own ideas. Anything that you think is valuable in making you a better person should be included and shared with others. Take these quotes that I am offering and don't just read them. Think about them, see if you agree with me.

Also just don't read quotes as fast as you can get through them. Take each one and consider it, live in it. Talk to your friends about it. The go on to the next quote. If you really like it write it down in your own journal. You do have a journal, don't you?

I was playing atmosphere music for a luncheon and a man walked up to me as said, "would you like to take my class on business and people for free in turn for playing music for our luncheon and dinner the next two days?" That turned out to be one of the most instructive and interesting two days of my life. The first thing he did was when everyone came into the banquet room was hand them a blank journal. I think my first journal is one-third filled with the genius of Jim Rohn.

Fear cannot exist in the present.
—Michael Anthony

GENERAL QUOTES

Don't think about the ball, be the ball.
—Michael Anthony

Writing about music is like dancing about architecture.
—Martin Mull

Sometimes a man must fight so hard for his life,
he doesn't have time to live it.
—Charles Bukowski

Common sense is not so common.
—Voltaire, 1764

Truth is the cry of all, but the game of few.
—George Berkeley, 1744

Even little white lies deny people their autonomy,
their ability to decide for themselves on the basis
of true facts. Lies are a means of coercion.
—Michael Josephson

The moral question is not: should we lie or tell the truth?
It is rather: To whom do we owe our honesty.
—Anonymous

Those who know don't talk.
Those who talk don't know.
—Lao Tzu

Honor is a gift a man gives himself.
—Ricky Gervais

Let no man pull you low enough to hate him.
—Martin Luther King, Jr.

He said, "Write it on your heart that every day is the best day in the year. He is rich who owns the day, and no one owns the day who allows it to be invaded with fret and anxiety. Finish every day and be done with it. You have done what you could. Some blunders and absurdities, no doubt crept in. Forget them as soon as you can, tomorrow is a new day; begin it well and serenely, with too high a spirit to be cumbered with your old nonsense. This new day is too dear, with its hopes and invitations, to waste a moment on the yesterdays."
—Ralph Waldo Emerson

Zenosyne: The sense that time keeps going faster.
—John Koenig, *The Dictionary of Obscure Sorrows*

Onism: The awareness of how little of the world you will experience.
—John Koenig, *The Dictionary of Obscure Sorrows*

Go with truth and beauty, and forget the rest.
—Bill Evans

Be a student of style The final outcome should be "your style."
—Jim Rohn

Still my personal favorite:
Save your money.
—Mike Vaccaro

A true friend can give help without
remembering they gave it.
And they can accept help without
forgetting where it came from.
—Dan Jacobs

The battle of being mortal
is the battle to maintain
the integrity of one's life.
—Atul Gawande,
Being Mortal: Medicine and What Matters in the End

One should keep their words soft and tender,
because tomorrow they may have to eat them.
—Andy Rooney

To ignore the facts,
does not change the facts.
—Andy Rooney

When you lose,
don't lose the lesson.
—Dalai Lama

Every time you get upset at something,
ask yourself if you were to die tomorrow,
was it worth your time getting angry?
—Robert Tew

Spend 20% of you time with people that waste your time,
and 80% of your time with people that you admire.
—Anonymous

BUSINESS QUOTES

Write your plan down!!! NOW!!!
Put it where you can see it every day.
Work the plan daily, and wait for your success.
—Mike Vaccaro

Educate yourself and we will need all your intelligence.
Be excited because we will need all your enthusiasm.
Organize because we will need all of your strength.
—Antonio Gramsci

Why let your attention get hijacked
by trivial matters beyond your control?
—Dan Jacobs, *The Natural Laws of Selling*

The master has failed more times
than the beginner has even tried.
—Stephen McCranie

Social Connections play a fundamental
role in a successful career.
—Isabele Allende

We make a living by what we get,
and we make a life by what we give.
—Winston Churchill

It takes as much time to chase the big money
as it does to chase the small money.
—Mike Vaccaro

MUSIC AND ART QUOTES

You must sing, if you wish to play.
—F. Chopin

Practice your craft one minute a day.
—Mike Vaccaro

An Artist is not paid for his labor,
but rather his vision.
—James Whistler

FOR MUSICIANS & ARTISTS

Walk lightly (be kind to all). But...
Carry a big stick (know your craft).
—Mike Vaccaro

Act as if what you do makes a difference.
It Does!!!
—William James

Chops are Chops
and Music is Music
A player can have both, however,
the goal is not to be the best,
but to give the music its own life.
—Mike Vaccaro

People that live only for themselves,
and not for others, are only half alive.
—Christiane Brahms

Melody is everything.
—Kevin Oviatt

Each of us has a unique life. For better or worse, it affects our whole being and our music. There are those lucky ones who grow up in a musical household. They have a better chance at success. For the rest of us, we must make it happen by something internal that demands that we play music or participate in the arts. There may be death, disease, or a myriad of other conditions that take us off the path. We must persevere and participate at whatever level we are able, always coming back to the path. For those that really want it, it's worth the ride.
—Mike Vaccaro

Human beings are, necessarily, actors who cannot become something before they have first pretended to be it; and they can be divided, not into the hypocritical and the sincere, but into the sane who know they are acting and the mad who do not.
—W. H. Auden

Laugh about the pain.
—Leoncavallo

The first sound after silence should always be your best. In a perfect world, every note would be your best, but the first sound after silence is the one that will be remembered.
—Arnold Jacobs – Chicago Symphony

Music is the silence between notes.
—Claude Debussy

A painter paints pictures on canvas.
But musicians paint their pictures on silence.
—Stokowski

The art of not playing in tempo—
one has to learn it.
—Pablo Casals

Courage doesn't always roar. Sometimes
courage is the quiet voice at the end of the
day saying, "I will try again tomorrow."
—Mary Anne Radmacher

You make your mistakes to learn
how to get to the good stuff.
—Quincy Jones

In music, silence is more important than sound.
—Miles Davis

The number one skill that all successful
musicians have mastered is not giving up.
—Anonymous

You only need to study music for a minute a day. Sounds
radical, doesn't it? The point is getting your instrument
out of the case, sitting down, calming down, forgetting all
the things that are pulling on you, and just getting started.
If you are interested at all, you can't just play one minute.
—Mike Vaccaro

To record yourself is to know yourself.
—Mike Vaccaro

Those who don't want to imitate anything produce nothing.
—Salvadore Dali

Forget you are being listened to
And always listen to yourself.
—Chopin

Its either going to be ok
or it's not going to be ok.
So just don't worry about it.
—Mike Vaccaro

While average is looking for an excuse,
exceptional is finding a way.
—Dan Jacobs

Success in the Arts
is tenuous at best.
—Anonymous

The meaning of life is to find your gift.
The purpose of life is to give it away.
—Pablo Picasso

If you want to be happy,
you have to be happy on purpose.
When you wake up, you can't wait to
see what kind of day you will have.
You have to decide what kind of day you will have.
—Joel Osteen

Learn the rules like a Pro,
so you can break them like an Artist.
—Pablo Picasso

SOME THOUGHTS FROM JIM ROHN

Experience translates into value.

*There is no better opportunity to receive more
than to be thankful for what you already have.*

Cynicism shuts the door to new ideas.

Be eager to learn.

*Don't take the casual approach to life.
Casualness leads to casualties. Seek out the mentors that
you need that will lead you to greatness in your field.
If you're not willing to learn from others,
who are you willing to learn from?*

*Learn how to turn frustration into fascination.
You will learn more being fascinated by life
than you will by being frustrated by it.*

Nothing works every time.

Have treasures of the mind.

Take notes.

Read because you must.

*If you really want to do something,
you'll find a way.
If you don't, you'll find an excuse*
—Jim Rohn

MORE GENERAL QUOTES

Luck will play a role in your life,
but it's not the part you expect.
It is still important to set up your plan,
and follow up with your contingency plan,
as luck will only carry you so far.
—Mike Vaccaro

Art is making a thing, and then
trying to make a better one.
And you keep doing that until you die,
and that's a pretty good life.
—Mike Vaccaro

Life is indeed terribly complicated—
to a man who has lost his principles.
—G.K. Chesterton

Have you ever noticed that listening and asking questions
might be more helpful than just giving your advice?
—Dan Jacobs

Your limitations stem from internal not external beliefs.
These are what put the brakes on your potential.
—Dan Jacobs

To be excellent at small things takes the same
amount of effort as be excellent at big things.
—Horoscope

There is honor in paying.
—Mike Vaccaro

About the Author

MIKE VACCARO has been very active in the classical, jazz, and pop music genres, performing and working in theater, opera, and motion picture productions, as well as orchestra and chamber music throughout his 60-year career.

Mike has also had many interests in the music business. He was the House Music Contractor at the Cerritos Center for thirty years and was a Union official for several years. He owned his own production company, producing celebrity concerts and serving as a talent agency.

During a lifetime in music, his most cherished memories were playing baritone sax with Stan Kenton and solo clarinet on *Ratatouille* as well as other Pixar movies. His chamber music trio "Musique" was the highlight of his career.

Over and above his music career, he has made improvements to the design of the clarinet and makes custom-made mouthpieces for clarinets, bass clarinets, and the sax.

He has been honored to record ten full-length CDs. Perhaps most importantly, Mike still likes to pay it forward by working with private students.

Printed in the USA
CPSIA information can be obtained
at www.ICGtesting.com
LVHW020550080923
757249LV00015B/181